Engaging Leaders

Addressing the question of how leadership can work most successfully in universities, *Engaging Leaders* strengthens the sense of shared professional knowledge and capability among leaders in higher education. Presenting a narrative of change, this book not only spells out why universities need to work differently, but also takes the reader through clear practical steps that any practising leader can take in order to build a collaborative professional culture that supports and challenges all members of an academic community.

Using a selection of case studies from UK and international universities, the book explores why working collectively remains a fundamental challenge for many higher education institutions and looks at the benefits of creating a collective commitment throughout universities. It covers:

- action learning and professional learning communities
- emotionally intelligent organizational cultures
- feedback as an intrinsic tool
- building partnerships and collaborations
- higher education and public value
- cultures of innovation and sustainable practices.

Engaging Leaders is for those who see themselves as leaders in higher education, whether or not this is recognized in their job title. It provides stimulating perspectives on what they might do to become more engaged and engaging, and includes examples of inspiring practice that is already making a difference in universities, colleges and new private providers. It will be of value to established managers as well as those new in post, and also for those participating in postgraduate programmes.

Paul Gentle is Director of Programmes at the Leadership Foundation for Higher Education, UK. He is also Programme Director for the *Top Management Programme*.

Dawn Forman is an adjunct professor at Curtin University and Auckland University of Technology and a visiting professor at Chichester University. She has published five books, 10 chapters and over 50 articles in peer-reviewed journals.

Engaging Leaders

The challenge of inspiring collective commitment in universities

Paul Gentle with Dawn Forman

Routledge
Taylor & Francis Group

LONDON AND NEW YORK

First published 2014
by Routledge
2 Park Square, Milton Park, Abingdon, Oxon OX14 4RN

and by Routledge
711 Third Avenue, New York, NY 10017

Routledge is an imprint of the Taylor & Francis Group, an informa business

© 2014 Paul Gentle with case studies by Dawn Forman

British Library Cataloguing in Publication Data
A catalogue record for this book is available from the British Library

Library of Congress Cataloging in Publication Data
Gentle, Paul.
  Engaging leaders : the challenge of inspiring collective commitment in
  universities / authored by Paul Gentle; with Dawn Forman.
    p. cm.
  Includes bibliographical references and index.
  ISBN 978-0-415-83817-7 (hbk : alk. paper)—ISBN 978-0-415-83818-4
  (pbk : alk. paper)—ISBN 978-1-315-79641-3 (ebk : alk. paper)
  1. Education, Higher—Administration.   2. Universities and colleges—
  Administration.   3. Educational leadership.   4. College administrators.
  5. Organizational change.   I. Forman, Dawn.   II. Title.
  LB2341.G46 2014
  378.1'11—dc23   2013038882

ISBN: 978-0-415-83817-7 (hbk)
ISBN: 978-0-415-83818-4 (pbk)
ISBN: 978-1-315-79641-3 (ebk)

Typeset in Galliard
by RefineCatch Limited, Bungay, Suffolk

Printed and bound in Great Britain by
TJ International Ltd, Padstow, Cornwall

This book is dedicated to the multitude of leaders who have taught me all the lessons that have shaped and continue to inform my practice.

Thanks to the Leadership Foundation for Higher Education for supporting me during the writing of the book, and to Cláudia Laranjeira for her wonderful work on the cover.

Paul Gentle

Contents

Foreword

Dr Mark Pegg
Chief Executive, Leadership Foundation
for Higher Education

Engaging Leaders investigates how leaders like you inspire and gain commitment from others to take on difficult challenges and build conditions in which people in universities can fulfil their potential. It offers practical advice for leaders called upon to create highly intelligent institutions for highly intelligent people. It focuses on things that keep leaders awake at night.

This book is for leaders of people who value personal space in individualistic cultures and who prize their own academic discipline and place their own freedoms above all: people who sometimes overlook the leaders that create the conditions whereby they are free to be innovative and creative. This is a book for leaders who want to learn how to engage with everyone in their academic and professional community and build a collaborative, high-performing culture.

The author is a skilled leadership developer, writing in a refreshingly insightful and accessible style. Paul Gentle challenges you to press the limits, to reach out further, and calls on you to turn ideas into action. These rapidly changing times call for new ways of thinking, new ways to bring people with you, to effect the sort of engagement that will enable real change in the culture. Paul shares his experience and insight to help you to effect transformational change in the institution you serve.

The book offers you in-depth thinking on each theme and backs this up in each chapter with contemporary case studies, researched and co-written by Dawn Forman, to inspire you and inform your approach to leadership. It supplements these case studies with useful practical resources to help you bring about changes in your own leadership practice. The thinking behind the book is based both on Paul Gentle's current research and ideas gained from the unique access he has to university leaders in the course of his work for the Leadership Foundation.

Paul knows his trade intimately and shares his tradecraft. As a tutor and director of programmes, he is rated consistently highly by his students in programme evaluations; he is one of the very best, a skilled professional, an all-rounder, with a rare combination of skills and experience. He knows the sector, draws on wider business experience, has classroom presence and can undertake research. This gives him huge credibility with participants from across the most senior levels in the UK's universities.

Paul and I work together at the Leadership Foundation, and I know that much of what you read in this book is tried and tested in his interaction with participants. He learns with them, shares their hopes and fears. He encourages people to learn more about their inner strengths and to find the courage to face up to the difficult conversations; to go through uncomfortable experiences and learn from them.

Engaging Leaders offers fresh thinking that will work for you. It will build your confidence to lead through engagement, to engender collaboration and commitment in your institution: the essentials for you as a successful leader of people in a world-class university.

Preface

A body of evidence points to a contemporary reality: in the face of unprecedented turbulence for some institutions, it seems rational for many senior figures in universities to resort to well-defined (yet frequently critiqued) management roles and associated toolkits for implementation. However, adopting such approaches often makes it problematic to engage with their own *leadership identity*. As a result, they miss opportunities to be engaging as *leaders*, and to engage others in securing the discretionary effort from all in the workforce to enable universities to transform lives, win public support and thrive.

The book aims to provide readers with stimulating perspectives on what they might do to become more engaged and engaging leaders.

Introduction

The first decade of the twenty-first century presented considerable challenges to those working in taxpayer-funded services, as relationships between the State and its citizens metamorphosed under the aegis of the public sector change agenda (Maddock, 2009). The current decade is witness to exponential growth in both the scale and the scope of those challenges.

Where professionals leading and managing in public sector activity – spanning health, policing, social care, higher education, public administration and schooling – are being urged to 'do more with less', they are also charged variously with responsibilities for *workforce engagement* (Macleod and Clarke, 2009), *strategic agility* (Doz and Kosonen, 2008) and, time and energy permitting, *paradigm innovation* (Bessant et al., 2010).

No longer can prescribed management solutions be wheeled into service, except in the most predictable or critically urgent situations (Grint, 2005, 2010). When faced with super-complex problems, those employed as professionals in the public education sector need more than ever to see themselves as leaders. Crucially, they also need to engender qualities of leadership among those surrounding them at all levels of the public bodies and institutions in which they work, and to ensure that they become the architects and designers of 'leaderful' organizations (Raelin, 2003, 2010).

The drivers of change in public sector organizations are not just the obvious ones of reducing costs, increasing efficiency and shedding expensive staff. It could be argued that these are actually levers for more profound change – change that entails a radical shift, away from a public sector that 'delivers' services, and towards what has been called 'the relational State' (Mulgan, 2010).

For those in higher education, adjusting to this change may prove challenging: not only intellectually, but emotionally (Kegan and Lahey, 2009). Never has the phrase 'winning hearts and minds' seemed so apt, in light of competitive challenges both inside and outside the sector. Strengthening leadership capability – and, importantly, followership capacity (Kellerman, 2012) – in our universities and university colleges is now, more than ever, imperative if we are to take colleagues with us on the change journeys now under way.

Academics have not always been demonstrably interested in how they were led. As recently as 2010, a survey reaffirmed a view that most academic staff felt a deeper, more meaningful sense of engagement with their disciplines and associated networks, in preference to affinity with their employing institutions. A set of cliché-ridden notions associated with the practical realities of working in universities is still arguably recognizable in some higher education practitioners: academics are autonomous professionals who cannot be managed (the 'herding cats' analogy); their status is equivalent to that of medical consultants or partners in a legal practice; success is measured by individual outputs and consequent reputation; applying a rigorous critical stance to one's work implies valuing cognitive intelligence above interpersonal relationships. These notions are being challenged by the *realpolitik* of institutions that need to change in order to thrive.

After a decade from 2000 to 2010 in which the importance of leadership in the public sector was recognized by policymakers through establishing a range of organizations with responsibility for leadership development in their respective sectors (such as defence, post-compulsory learning, schools, local government), a growing sense of the positive impact of leadership emerged (Cabinet Office, 2009).

In the United Kingdom, the Leadership Foundation for Higher Education (Leadership Foundation), set up in 2004 following a government White Paper (Department for Education and Skills, 2003), has played its part, as we will see later. It has actively supported a network of Organizational Development practitioners across the university sector, and this grouping could claim to have influenced institutional change significantly. Through its bespoke provision and open programmes of leadership development, it has helped to establish an emergent community of practice among professional university leaders. The Leadership Foundation has become the envy of higher education systems across the globe, and has responded to the absence of equivalent bodies in other countries by expanding its activities internationally. Significantly, it has taken the decision not to undertake such an expansion single-handedly, but through leveraging the collaborative energy and capacity of a range of strategic partner organizations. In other words, the Leadership Foundation is finding success in its expansion through realizing the power of *collective commitment* (Bolden et al., 2008).

In this book, we will explore how individual leaders in universities, wherever they may be located in geographical or hierarchical terms, might rise to the challenge of inspiring commitment in others.

This book is intended to strengthen the sense of shared professional knowledge and capability among leaders in higher education. It presents a narrative of change that not only spells out why universities need to work differently, but also takes the reader through clear practical steps which any practising leader can take in order to build a professional culture that is collaborative and engages all members of an academic community.

Possibilities for leadership

An evaluation of the Leadership Foundation in 2010 (HEFCE, 2010a) concluded that leadership and management careers were seen as increasingly desirable by many working in higher education, and that 84% of staff in the higher education sector value leadership alongside academic prestige.

A high proportion of those appointed to the most senior leadership positions in higher education are alumni of Leadership Foundation programmes, and in particular its flagship *Top Management Programme*. One could expect that a shared discourse of leadership might by now permeate the universities and university colleges of the UK. To date, relatively little evidence is available against which to test such speculation. In other nations, evidence of sophistication in leadership in higher education is similarly scarce. Time and again, those with recognized strengths in other significant aspects of higher education activity (particularly in research) are promoted into positions in which effective leadership is critical, but for which they are arguably given insufficient support.

Kennie and Woodfield (2008) note that even in senior management groupings, classic dysfunctions can undermine successful team working. Gibbs et al. (2009) observe that individual academic departmental heads see their leadership through a widely differing set of conceptual prisms – with what one might presume to be a widely varying set of effects on those working in their departments.

A body of evidence points to a contemporary reality: in the face of impending crisis for some institutions, many senior figures in universities find it more intuitive (and sometimes politically convenient) to resort to well-defined (and frequently critiqued) management roles and associated toolkits for implementation. They find it much more difficult to engage with their own identity and that of their colleagues as leaders. As a result, they miss opportunities to be engaging as leaders, and to engage others in securing the discretionary effort from all in the workforce to enable universities to transform lives, win public support and thrive.

This book is for those who see themselves as leaders, whether or not this is recognized in their job title. It aims to build on earlier work on leadership in higher education (Middlehurst, 1993; McCaffery, 2010) and to provide stimulating perspectives on what they might do to become more engaged and engaging, and to include some examples of inspiring practice that is already making a difference in universities and university colleges. The challenge will be for those who find these perspectives worthwhile to make them work in their own contexts, and in doing so to advance the sense of belonging to a growing professional community of practice (Wenger, 1998) of higher education leaders.

At this point, it may worth making a clear statement on the values, propositions and beliefs about leadership that have informed my own experience as a leader and leadership developer, and that are central to this book. These are as follows.

- Participatory decision-making is a key facet of effective leadership in higher education (Bryman, 2007: 2), together with 'fostering a supportive and collaborative environment'.
- Collective learning is critical to developing organizational learning, as supported by Belbin's view (2010: 72) that 'the mature team can be gauged by its learning'.

- Change can be led and managed proactively through deliberate cultivation of leadership at all levels of an organization (Fullan, 2001: x).
- 'Personal authenticity' is essential in leaders. This derives (West-Burnham and Ireson, 2005: 18) from the overlap and connectedness between cognitive and affective literacy (the ability to dialogue meaningfully with self and others), moral and spiritual values, and action: 'Leadership development might . . . be seen as the process of becoming personally authentic'.
- Leadership of collaborative working cultures pays attention to creating a lasting, sustainable legacy (Hargreaves and Harris, 2011). It is not about dependency on a single heroic individual or grouping.
- The quality of discourse manifest in how a university conducts its leadership, governance and management activities is crucial in determining the extent to which members of the workforce feel empowered. Among barriers to such enabling discourse are cultures of deference (Ryde, 2013) and the power distance associated with hierarchies (Hofstede, 1980).

When the working culture of a professional community can change through implementing such values in daily practice, then the full extent of the possibilities for leadership might begin to be realized.

Barriers and enablers

In strategic terms, universities seek competitive advantage through distinctive capabilities: the extent to which mission, innovation, reputation and location enable higher education institutions to position themselves has become crucial to the sense of diversity between institutions, and to student choice. The inducement given to higher education institutions to reform, through increasing tuition fees and reducing the direct public contribution (DBIS, 2010c, 2011), while simultaneously introducing mechanisms that accelerate market openness, is arguably leading to stronger differentiation, positioning and branding.

Innovation might be expressed in terms of teaching, learning and assessment approaches, curriculum design, employer engagement, student-centred service provision, staff development, and – not to be overlooked – approaches to management and leadership.

The headlong rush towards renewed focus on 'the student experience' might be seen to play into the hands of those who would conceive of higher education as part of the service industries. However, Nayar (2010) suggests that the common business wisdom of putting customers first without attending to the needs of the workforce is an example of failed strategy.

Reputation, as measured in published 'league tables', is usually taken in higher education to refer to institutions' quality and standards, student achievement and satisfaction, research output, and graduate employability. Accountability for performance indicators in all these areas is usually vested in middle managers such as Deans and Heads of Department, and any attempt to lead staff in order to produce improvements depends on the strategic and operational decisions taken by these leaders (Harvey and Knight, 1996).

The dichotomy between 'command and control' and collaborative working, which is frequently manifested among senior and middle layers of management in higher education institutions (Ramsden, 1998; Harvey and Knight, 1996), is crucial to the organizational cultures of higher education institutions – and frequently acts as a barrier to realizing true organizational learning.

For middle managers such as departmental heads, there is often considerable tension resulting from feeling answerable both upwards and downwards within the university. Bryman (2007: 5) describes them as 'hemmed in by a pincer movement of senior management and academic staff'.

While the literature readily identifies the above factors as barriers to bringing about collective commitment in universities, it also provides a rich range of examples of enablers of changed and changing practices. Included here are Fullan's concepts of knowledge creation and sharing across an organization, and of the importance of distributed leadership. Of particular interest to Fullan is the causal relationship between collaborative work cultures and knowledge sharing, which he characterizes as: 'slow knowing and learning in context with others at all levels of the organization' (2001: 137).

Although Fullan makes no reference to the work of Revans (1983) or of Senge (1990), he is clearly talking about achieving similar ends: 'your leadership in a culture of change will be judged as effective . . . *by what leadership you produce in others*' (2001: 137; emphasis in original).

Thinkers in educational leadership have posited the challenge of creating, developing and sustaining a 'professional learning community' as a 'major strategic leadership and management task' (NCSL, 2006: 8). Such a community is recognizable by a shared learning vision and supportive, inquiry-based working which is focused on professional practice.

Bryman (2007) identifies a gap between the emphasis in school leadership thinking on distributed leadership and any take-up of this concept in higher education. One reason may lie with perceived difficulties of distributed leadership as a true embodiment of democracy (Woods, 2003). Another may be that it could be seen as at odds with the increasingly accountability-driven world in which higher education institutions have found themselves (Zepke, 2007).

Bryman points to the bias in research on leadership in higher education (2007: 17) in emphasizing 'outcomes for employees rather than students', and hence its overlooking of the impact of effective leadership on the student learning experience. This aspect is addressed more fully by Gibbs et al. (2009: 2), who stress the importance of dispersed leadership in research-intensive university departments that are 'demonstrably excellent at teaching'. Several of the case examples offered in their study 'involve a comprehensive planned innovation to address an identified problem', and call on a range of characteristics of what might be termed collaborative organizational cultures, including:

- establishing credibility and trust
- building a community of practice
- supporting change and innovation
- involving students.

Anderson highlights the need for alignment between pedagogical and leadership paradigms, echoing a contemporary educational theme of managers as leaders of learning in an inclusive sense:

> Leading and managing people and teams in educational organisations is not only about applying these functions to the staff and volunteers who work within the organisation, it is also about leading and managing the learners who are registered with the educational establishment.
>
> (2003: 12)

Faced with the challenges of demonstrating the value to students of higher tuition fees from 2012–13, finding – or perhaps reinventing – such a sense of alignment would appear to be a worthwhile strategic aim for many contemporary higher education providers.

Chapter 1 of this book explores in greater detail the underlying issues that explain why working collectively remains a fundamental challenge for many higher education institutions. Chapter 2 sets out a case for the benefits of achieving collective commitment in our universities.

Approaches to developing leaders

Leadership development programmes, such as those offered by the Leadership Foundation, are often presented as enablers to collective learning. They frequently incorporate approaches such as action learning, which participants seem very largely to find helpful and rewarding – but it seems to be left there, in the programme, and is rarely applied to senior management activity within the participants' own institutions.

One rare example of discussion of the extent to which action learning contributes to organizational learning in higher education can be found in work by Passfield (2002). He attributes the success of an institution-wide programme of action learning for senior academic and administrative staff of the University of Queensland in the 1990s to the concept of its being a 'parallel learning structure' (since it coexisted with formal notions of hierarchical leadership), and claims benefits in terms of 'increased capacity to collaborate, as well as improved working relationships' (2002: 155).

Action learning will be explored further in Chapter 3, alongside other enablers of successful group dynamics. Chapter 4 focuses on applying emotional intelligence to designing opportunities for engagement, including approaches for reconceptualizing meetings and similar gatherings. Chapter 5 examines how giving and seeking feedback is intrinsic to practices and behaviours throughout an organizational unit.

Chapter 6 is devoted to enabling institutions to develop systemic cultures of innovation that support agile, strategic working. Finally, Chapter 7 challenges leaders in higher education to influence beyond their institutional boundaries in order to build successful external partnerships and collaborations.

Each section of this book offers case study examples to illustrate current and future practice in universities in Europe, North America and Asia Pacific.

Terminology used in this book

This book is intended to be used by leaders of all kinds, in a diverse range of institutions of higher education around the world. This range includes large universities in both public and private hands, specialist institutions such as conservatoires, agricultural colleges and medical institutes, as well as a huge variety of locally focused providers of tertiary education.

In using the terms 'university' and 'institution', the intention of the authors is not to preclude the wider range of providers; these terms serve as shorthand to indicate the full diversity of higher education sectors in different countries.

Each chapter offers a number of *case studies* that are designed to shed light on the chapter topics, focusing on institutions in various parts of the world that exemplify relevant leadership practice. Each case study includes questions that are intended to stimulate reflection and discussion, particularly when this book is used as part of a programme of study or of leadership development.

Most chapters also offer *resources* that can be used as practical tools by leaders interested in broadening their professional practice, particularly where strengthening collective commitment to action is concerned.

We welcome feedback on the extent to which readers find the case studies and resources helpful and practical in supporting their work, and wish you success in making changes in your working cultures.

1 Universities and individualism

Academic and leadership identities
Why working collectively remains a fundamental challenge for many higher education institutions

As the prelude to an interview process for a senior institutional role in the past decade, I was taken around the building where I might eventually be working. This exponent of early twenty-first century university architecture offered incontestably the most stunning view in the city; a view that would have been a memorable highlight of the day, had it not been for what I was shown on two of its floors.

These were not the floors housing the user-friendly faculty administration, nor those with state-of-the-art teaching and learning facilities and spaces for students to meet and relax. Sandwiched between all of these were two floors that contained a vast uninhabited tundra of desks, filing cabinets and dividing screens. Across some three thousand square feet, I counted a handful of souls, none of whom even glanced up from their work stations.

'And these,' said the Faculty Marketing Assistant who was my guide, without a hint of irony, 'are the academic floors. But nobody ever comes in, 'cause they don't like it – so they always work from home.'

The challenge of influencing this invisible cohort of two hundred academics suddenly became crystal clear, and I subsequently turned down the post that the university offered me.

On reflection, it struck me that not one person in what would have been my 'team' had their own office, and furthermore that the building had expressly been designed so as to facilitate communication and co-operation. What had gone wrong?

Later in the day, I heard much about the need to improve the research output of individual staff, to drive up economic efficiency and to develop the enterprise agenda. I couldn't help wondering which of these priorities the absent staff felt they had signed up to, and which they might most successfully be able to work on at a distance. It certainly didn't seem as though the faculty's work was essentially social or collaborative, or that people derived a sense of purpose from belonging to it as an organization.

This will not surprise many readers. The tension between individual professional autonomy and collaborative working is well documented in the higher education literature:

> It's really hard to get people to understand why collaboration is so important and that these are higher-order skills they need to acquire. They can acknowledge this intellectually, but every fibre in their body (and their experience, and history) is pointing diametrically in the other direction.
>
> (Garrett and Davies, 2010: 36)

The pressures towards collaborative working are multiple, and highly complex. For a range of reasons connected to academic identity (Bolden et al., 2012), such pressures are often resisted using a counter-corporate rhetoric. In a *tour de force* of deconstructing the paradigm of the managed institution, Collini notes the longstanding ideal of regarding the university as a public good, which 'entails a certain kind of withdrawal from society's everyday activities, an indication of a concern with considerations that are longer term and less material' (2012: 86).

Nevertheless, Collini also observes that 'life in universities is now *less unlike* life in other large organizations than at any time in the long history [of universities]' (2012: 18; emphasis in original). This practical reality brings with it a raft of associated questions about how much can be learnt about leading and managing organizations from other sectors; furthermore, from which other sectors might we wish to learn?

Interesting parallels can be drawn between other sectors with strong paradigms of individual professional autonomy, such as medicine, public service broadcasting journalism and legal practice.

There is much evidence to support the view that in the first part of the twenty-first century, universities have become highly effective organizations, and that in becoming so, many could claim to rival the commercial prowess and acumen of successful businesses. Many vice-chancellors and presidents rightly pride themselves on the extent to which they have steered their universities through turbulence to levels of success that not only are acknowledged by their peers, but also are praised by cabinet ministers, captains of industry and heads of cultural institutions. Indeed in the United Kingdom, one exemplar of all of these can be found in the role of Chief Executive in some individual providers of higher education. At the same time, many businesses, especially in the knowledge industries, aspire to being more like universities in terms of their ethos and working culture.

Yet all is not necessarily as well as it might be. Watson (2009) explores the extent to which the contemporary university is characterized by unhappiness, and starts by asserting that the immediate response from a typical individual working in a university to a question on what morale is like will probably be 'At rock bottom!'

In rushing to demonstrate their ability to adapt to circumstances and transform their institutions accordingly, there is the risk that university leaders may not have taken public opinion with them. In many Western nations, for instance, the idea of the university as a public and social good may have lost some of its lustre. Politicians' rhetoric is not always helpful in this respect, invoking the responsibilities of higher education to lead economies out of recession and into growth, or to upskill the workforces of the present and future. There is the danger that an instrumental purpose for universities begins to dominate the prevailing discourse.

This leads to the notion of taxpayers questioning the value for money offered by universities, to individual students, their parents, employers and a raft of other stakeholders. It detracts from questions of deeper educational value, of transformational learning which has the power to change people's lives, and of the cultural and social missions that are the lifeblood of our institutions.

Collini (2012) has attempted to address this shift in perception, calling for a re-examination of the wider value offered by universities, and questions the notions of 'excellence' and 'student satisfaction' around which the management of universities often appears to revolve. Collini questions what has prevailed until recently as the benchmark for universities – 'the nineteenth-century European ideal' – and asks whether 'it is the Asian incarnation of the Americanized version of the European model, with schools of technology, medicine, and management to the fore, which most powerfully instantiates the idea of the university in the twenty-first century' (2012: 13).

The onus is now on authentic leaders in our universities to rise to the challenge of asserting the rights and responsibilities of universities in modelling the change we would wish to see in the world around us. A useful starting point might be to consider how we perceive ourselves, individually and collectively, as leaders.

In this book, all discussion of the work of leaders is intended to have an inclusive focus. There is no assumption that leaders are only found high up in institutional hierarchies – rather, it is taken as read that leadership is a quality that potentially suffuses all aspects of the work of universities and colleges. If all students and staff are seen as – and most importantly, involved as though they are – part of a collective leadership effort, there are enormous possibilities for enriching and sustaining our institutions.

Rooke and Torbert shed some interesting light on the matter of leadership identities. Their concept of 'action logics' – 'how [leaders] interpret their surroundings and react when their power or safety is challenged' (2005: 3) – goes some way to explaining some of the fundamental gulfs in mindsets and behaviours that can play out in universities.

The authors define seven action logics into which leadership practitioners fall on the basis of a sentence-completion survey tool. These action logics are characterized in Table 1.1, together with a commentary on their prevalence in higher education institutions.

The narrative of Rooke and Torbert's article (2005: 5) provides further exemplification of leadership behaviours in action. On reflecting on my own career as a leader in higher education, it strikes me that at one particular stage I made an unintentional transition – at least in one area of my job role – from the Achiever to the Individualist action logic, the catalyst for which was the appointment of a new Chief Executive at the institution in which I was working.

Table 1.1 Action logics in the context of higher education; adapted from Rooke and Torbert (2005)

Action logic	Characteristics	Strengths	% of research sample profiling at this action logic	Likely manifestation in universities
Opportunist	Wins any way possible. Self-oriented; manipulative; 'might makes right'.	Good in emergencies and in sales opportunities	5	Depending on selection processes used by institutions, there is a possibility that some very senior leaders may be in this category. Comes across initially as charismatic and 'visionary'.
Diplomat	Avoids overt conflict. Wants to belong; obeys group norms; rarely rocks the boat.	Good as supportive glue within an office; helps bring people together.	12	When opportunists are the dominant figures on teams, if they are surrounded by diplomats this is likely to contribute to deferential patterns of behaviour. In this case there may be a surface appearance of consensus in the group.
Expert	Rules by logic and expertise. Seeks rational efficiency.	Good as an individual contributor.	38	Academics and some professional services leaders are commonly found in this category. Where measurement of success is through individual performance, experts thrive. This action logic fits with a public discourse based on rationale and reason, as is often found in universities.
Achiever	Meets strategic goals. Effectively achieves goals through teams; juggles managerial duties and market demands.	Well suited to managerial roles; action- and goal-oriented.	30	'Career' leaders are likely to identify themselves in this grouping. This might include departmental heads, service directors, and faculty managers.

Individualist	Interweaves competing personal and organizational action logics. Creates unique structures to resolve gaps between strategy and performance.	10	Effective in venture and consulting roles.	Academics with skill in external engagement may well be in this category, along with others who see themselves as leaders that model an enterprise culture. Individualists may be seen as operating at the margins of the university.
Strategist	Generates organizational and personal transformations. Exercises the power of mutual inquiry, vigilance, and vulnerability for both the short and long terms.	4	Effective as a transformational leader.	Leaders with a self-confident, mature sense of their own leadership identity will aspire to being in this grouping. Faced with short-term pressures, strategists nevertheless manage to find the space and energy to focus on opportunities for learning and development. Effective executive Deans and other senior management team members would be in this grouping.
Alchemist	Generates social transformations. Integrates material, spiritual and societal transformation.	1	Good at leading society-wide transformations.	Exemplary senior leaders, including some outstanding vice-chancellors and presidents, are able to realize the full potential of their office and of their institutions to shape a sustainable future for the communities in which they interact, and for society at large. These colleagues live out the answers to the question 'What are universities for?'

This provided an insight into the potential threat that I appeared to represent, in the work for which I was responsible in international education, to some of my fellow senior managers in the institution. Individualists, for instance, demonstrate 'awareness of a possible conflict between their principles and their actions, or between the organization's values and its implementation of those values. This conflict becomes the source of tension, creativity, and a growing desire for further development' (Rooke and Torbert, 2005: 5). This helps to explain my increasing interest at the time in using action learning as a source of development, and in engaging in a wide range of leadership development activities.

However, there are negative aspects of this particular action logic: 'Individualists also tend to ignore rules they regard as irrelevant, which often makes them a source of irritation to both colleagues and bosses' (Rooke and Torbert, 2005: 5).

Further detail is given in an example of a female executive who 'formed a highly cohesive team within budget and . . . ahead of schedule . . . [however, she] had a reputation within the wider organization as a wild card. Although she showed great political savvy when it came to her individual projects, she put many people's noses out of joint . . . because of her unique, unconventional ways of operating . . . [and] her failure to acknowledge key organizational processes'(Rooke and Torbert, 2005: 5).

This mirrors my own experience in the institution, as far as relationships with senior managers were concerned. The seven action logics also offered an explanation as to the strikingly contrasting perceptions that senior managers had of the other main component of my job role – directing business and community engagement in the institution. Here I was seen not only as successful as a leader, but also to some extent as a role model. I was applying, again unintentionally, a different logic – that of Strategists, who: 'focus on organizational constraints and perceptions, which they treat as discussable and transformable . . . [they] are highly effective change agents' (Rooke and Torbert 2005: 5).

It is therefore understandable that senior managers found it difficult to reconcile my apparent resistance to desired change, as defined by themselves, in the international aspect of my portfolio.

Rooke and Torbert (2005: 9) pay considerable attention to processes of transition from one action logic to another. To move from the Expert to Achiever orientations, which is likely to be a key transition, for instance, for those taking on a new leadership role such as a departmental headship:

> speaking and listening must come to be experienced not as necessary, taken-for-granted ways of communicating predetermined ideas but as intrinsically forward-thinking, creative actions. Achievers use inquiry to determine whether they (and the teams and organization to which they belong) are accomplishing their goals and how they might accomplish them more effectively . . . plans that set new goals, are generated through probing and trusting conversation, are actively supported through executive coaching . . . [and] can be critical enablers at this point.

The understanding derived from the action logics reinforces the proposition that change at departmental level is likely to be effective if it is conceived as team-based, and that a key focus for team activity should be on learning itself.

Readers may wish to consider the transitions to Strategist and beyond. Rooke and Torbert make it clear that leadership development for emergent Strategists and Alchemists is distinct from that needed for the other action logics, in that it calls for mutual mentoring with peers in their networks. Such mentoring supports processes of collaborative inquiry; we shall refer frequently in this book to processes and resources that enable meaningful dialogue and inquiry, and one of the necessary characteristics for rigorous inquiry is that of challenging assumptions and embedded behaviours and practices. Those responsible for designing experiences that are intended to develop leadership in individuals and in groups, such as the Leadership Foundation, are able to incorporate practices of collaborative inquiry within programmes that they design. Nevertheless, the resources and activities provided in this book are intended for use by practising leaders in their day–to-day work.

Change in an institution is also only likely to be effective when it is linked to changing leaders' behaviour, and to preparedness by leaders at all levels of the institution to reflect openly, critically and constructively on the extent to which they can help to develop one another's strengths through working collaboratively and authentically. Learning how to do this, and examining what leaders can do to improve capacities in this respect, will be the focus of the rest of the book.

The corporate agenda
Are we really all in this together?

Research carried out by Bolden et al. (2012) during a difficult period in universities, when a 'perfect storm' of conditions contributed to a turbulent environment (in 2011 and 2012), showed the separation that existed between the respective mental conceptions held by academic staff in universities of academic leadership and of corporate management. The former is seen as being modelled by those who engender respect among a professional peer community, often because of their capability across a range of activities associated with academic leadership. These include mentoring junior academics as they embark on research careers, being seen as influential in their disciplinary field, having a network of current and potential collaborators, and leading by example in winning research funding. Interestingly, the activities cited did not refer to demonstrating excellence in teaching and learning support as being among the attributes of good academic leadership – and this survey covered a wide range of institutions, not only 'research-intensive' universities. The typical role exemplar of this kind of academic leadership is likely to be that of research professor.

By contrast, the conception of academic management was linked to co-ordinating administrative tasks internal to the functioning of the department, such as timetabling or handling budgets, as well as to representing the department in decision-making processes concerning strategic working in the context of the wider university.

Perceptions of those interviewed from a wide range of institutions were that the role that embodied a linkage between these two conceptions was that of Head of Department. This was seen as a sometimes thankless job to take on, in that it involves mediation between two different worlds – those of the discipline-focused academic functions associated with teaching and research, and of the managed intentions of the institution in realizing strategic goals and objectives. On one hand, the Head of Department can be seen as a shield, protecting departmental colleagues from the 'impositions' of the university's managerialist cultures and its associated bureaucratic procedures. On the other, the Head might be seen as a 'corporate lackey', serving the purposes of the institution and running the risk of alienation from the colleagues they are supposed to represent. In both cases, these perceptions cast the role in an unenviable light.

However, the researchers found that effective academic managers could support and enable academic leadership if they were able to give attention to the organizational climates for which they were responsible. Before examining these findings in more detail, it is worth setting them against the background of work carried out by Bryman (2007) on the characteristics of effective Heads of Department.

Bryman identified seven examples of behaviours on the part of university managers that were 'likely to cause damage' (2007: 3), namely:

- failing to consult
- not respecting existing values
- actions that undermine collegiality
- not promoting the interests of those for whom the leader is responsible
- being uninvolved in the life of the department/institution
- undermining autonomy
- allowing the department/institution to drift. (2007: 27)

Bolden et al. reinforce many of these characteristics, asserting three broad categories of ways in which Heads can contribute to enabling academic leadership, and thus potentially increase the extent of motivation among the workforce. These are:

(a) provide and protect an environment that enables productive academic work
(b) develop and support a sense of shared academic values and identity
(c) accomplish 'boundary spanning' on behalf of individuals and work groups.

Attention to factors of the organization's culture and climate is, of course, equally important for leaders of professional services in universities as for academic leaders. Let us explore some of the implications behind each of these factors.

A productive, enabling environment

There is a dimension here of the Head as someone who takes on bureaucratic tasks on behalf of academic colleagues and thus undertakes necessary but cumbersome organizational work. There is also a clear implication of shielding and protecting colleagues from the ambitions of the corporate institution, which are sometimes perceived as antipathetic to the interests of academics. As a result, the Head of Department has a challenging role mediating a wide range of differing sets of priorities. Nevertheless, an enabling environment can only enable as long as it is operationally viable, and securing motivation and consequent action from departmental staff is essential in order to support functions of marketing, finance, quality assurance and so on, which contribute to the viability of the department. A productive environment must surely be seen through a variety of different perspectives (not solely one of 'I must be free to pursue what I want'), and will ultimately involve a set of trade-offs. The negotiating, brokering capabilities of the Head will be crucial in reaching mutually beneficial outcomes. The leadership lessons that can be learnt as a Head of Department act as a crucible for developing leadership identity, and serve those who succeed well in preparing them for greater strategic responsibility if they wish to develop further careers in leading in higher education.

It is important not to underestimate the part that can be played by Heads of Department in shaping the educational experiences offered by the different disciplines involved. As Gibbs et al. (2009) identified, the way in which a Head understands the management and leadership of learning and teaching is critical in determining the culture in which relationships between students and staff are formed – and to the depth and quality of engagement that ensues.

The contemporary higher education institution can often seem like a universe of microcosmic organizations which interact in ways that are fundamentally different from how they might coexist as, for instance, subsidiaries of a commercial enterprise. There are arguably palpable limits to the extent to which it is possible to manage entire institutions in a rational and focused manner, despite the rhetoric of senior managers and corporate planners. Nevertheless, observers have noted for at least two decades the steady evolution of many institutions away from collegial behaviours to working towards more corporate approaches (McNay, 1995). Writing to this effect, Savin-Baden (2000) underlines the challenges faced by Heads of Department in serving multiple interests:

> The university has adopted an enterprise culture overall and is seeking to sustain this through a view of leadership that is seen as a group function within a changing organization . . . At departmental level there is a head of department who sees himself [*sic*] as a chief executive, who espouses corporate values and who has adopted a matrix structure in order to encourage innovative and adaptive behaviour in the staff. This means that a large and often fragmented department . . . can be team driven and transcend subject specialism. Yet . . . the matrix structure does not work.

Instead, the department is undermined through conflicts between subject and team loyalties.

Savin-Baden goes on to cite an example of a change initiative that failed because it was 'a team remit subsequently destroyed by subject-based agenda' (2000: 142). Herein lies the challenge for the university leader who wishes to challenge the prevailing culture.

CASE STUDY 1: THE UNIVERSITY OF BIRMINGHAM
Cultural change

Background

Professor David Eastwood became Vice-Chancellor at the University of Birmingham in April 2009. He had previously been Chief Executive of the Higher Education Funding Council for England and, therefore, was in a prime position to know about the multiplicity of changes that were affecting the sector. He had also been a member of the Browne independent review of higher education funding and student finance.

Following his arrival, the university developed a new strategic plan and alongside this sought to ensure that leadership development was enhanced across the university. In order to facilitate embedding the priorities of the university and the necessary changes in culture to facilitate this, a review of the present culture was undertaken using the Cultural Web (Johnson et al., 2008). This was reviewed by the delegates on a leadership development programme who both modified the model from their perspective of the current culture existing in the university and also indicated the culture they believed the university was trying to achieve and, therefore, what they, as leaders within the university, would be aiming towards.

The Cultural Web facilitates a review of the aspects considered to form the culture of an organization. Taking each in turn:

- **Stories** of the history of the institution, how loyalties are derived, stories of misdemeanours or how the institution gained its reputation are often provided here.
- **Symbols** are how the institution has come to be known: the red brick of a traditional university, or 'the building on the hill', a specific feature of a building, or the academic gowns may be seen to be a symbol.
- **Power structures:** These are often the line management structures within a university but could also relate to the power of certain individuals if they wield their authority more than the position would normally give rise to. Additionally, power could lie with the unions in some organizations.

- **Organizational structures:** Often within a university these relate to schools or faculties and to departmental support functions. Hierarchies may exist within such schools or departments and indeed between such departments.
- **Control systems:** Financial and quality assurance control mechanisms are generally highlighted here but, in addition, planning systems or bureaucratic mechanisms can be included.
- **Rituals and routines** relate to the way in which things are done within the university, protocols that are followed, communication mechanisms, committee relationships, the way promotions are undertaken, etc.
- **The paradigm** brings all of these aspects together. What does the summation of these aspects tell you about the culture of the organization as a whole?

Figure 1.1 provides an interpretation of the Cultural Web from the perspective of delegates on the leadership development programme as they perceived the culture to be at the time of their programme. Figure 1.2 shows the University of Birmingham Cultural Web as projected for 2016.

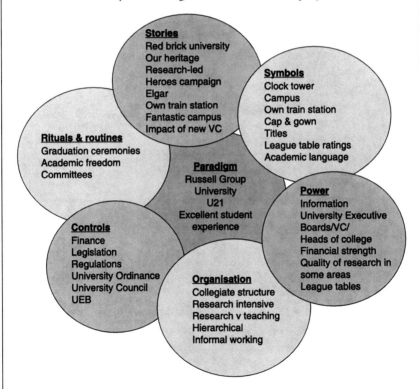

Figure 1.1 Cultural Web in 2011

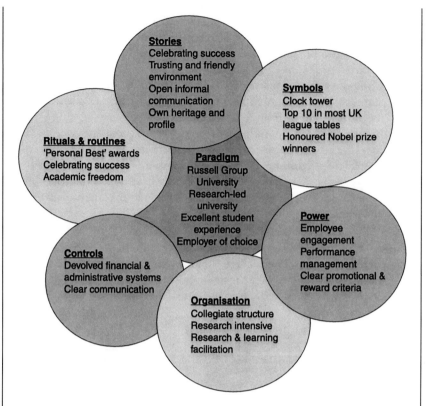

Figure 1.2 Cultural Web projected for 2016

Questions

1   Does your institution use a model like this to examine its culture and plan through cultural change?
2   What is the scope and scale of the cultural change you envisage taking place at the University of Birmingham?
3   Go through the exercise of creating each circle now for your institution.
4   Imagine your institution in five years' time. What would be different in each of the outer circles? How would the central paradigm be described?

The case study was developed by Kate Crane, University of Birmingham, and Professor Dawn Forman.

Developing and supporting shared values

Success here depends not so much on debate or discussion of values as on the extent to which they are seen to be lived out by leaders. If there is misalignment between espoused values and those observed through actions, it will prove very difficult to establish a climate of trust. Bluntly, if your institution declares that it values inclusivity (for example), but all decisions are taken by an elite group without reference to others, people will not believe in the stated values. Rather than declaring a set of values that appear to appeal to the sensibilities of those in educational institutions, it might first be worth investigating what people perceive to be the lived-out values of the institution, before seeing how these could be strengthened as appropriate.

Identifying your own values is an important starting point, as this will then enable you to assess your leadership behaviours at work in terms of the extent to which they apply your values. Using repertory grid techniques might help you to prioritize what you value most in yourself and in others.

RESOURCE 1: REPERTORY GRID

Stage 1

Make a set of eight blank cards for yourself; they should be easy to handle and shuffle as you work through the following activity.

On each of the first three cards, write down the name of a person whom you particularly admire; this could be someone you know well, such as a family member, friend or colleague, or a public figure you have not necessarily ever met.

On each of the next three cards, write the name of a person you categorically do not admire.

On the last two cards, write respectively 'Me Now' and 'Me Future'. The last of these refers to an aspirational view of how you would like to see yourself at some point in the future; this clearly assumes that a developmental process is possible to envisage, and that you are prepared to commit over a period of time to changing your own behaviour and actions.

Stage 2

Turn the cards face down, and shuffle them as a pack. Deal the top three cards to yourself, and turn them face up. As you look at the combination of the three people now revealed, organize them so that you can identify a characteristic that two of the people have in common, but the third does not. For example, if your cards are for 'Me Now', 'My grandmother' and 'My current boss', it may be that you identify 'providing direct, constructive feedback' as a characteristic of both your boss and your grandmother, but not of yourself.

Having identified the salient characteristic (Openness in giving constructive feedback), write this down in the Constructs column in the table.

After shuffling the pack carefully on each occasion, go through several more combinations of three cards until your list of constructs is full.

Stage 3

Assess yourself against these constructs using the columns on the right of the table. Note that there may be a gap between how you rate yourself for the present and the future. In the example given above, if I became aware that I was poor at giving direct and constructive feedback, yet wished to develop this as a lived-out behaviour, my ratings might be 3 (Now) and 8 (Future), depending on how strong a priority I felt it was to develop in this aspect.

Constructs	Ratings: Max = 10	
	Now	Future
1.		
2.		
3.		
4.		
5.		
6.		
7.		
8.		
9.		
10.		

Stage 4

Using the categories below, reflect on the implications for your own self-development.

Strengths:

Development needs:

With acknowledgement to Jan Hennessey, who facilitates this activity so well.

Many universities invest time in reflecting on their shared institutional values and how these might be manifested in the behaviours of the staff and students. In order to avoid cynical reactions from those working in the institution, it is of paramount importance that the lived-out behaviours of leaders align with the stated values of the institution.

Getting this right can make a huge difference in motivating people to work towards meaningful goals, and to contribute considerable amounts of what organizational psychologists call 'discretionary effort' – choosing to contribute above and beyond what is required contractually.

Boundary spanning

All university departments have representational needs that span boundaries, classically expressed in faculty committees, institution-wide working parties, membership of Academic Boards, and so on. Given the increasing emphasis on intra- and inter-institutional collaboration, there are likely to be many opportunities to span boundaries through partnership working. Not everybody is good at this, but leaders need to ensure it becomes part of their 'DNA', and need to build skills in developing others to be effective boundary spanners (see Chapter 7 for more specific ideas on how you might approach this).

Later chapters will focus on the practical steps leaders can take to build the climate and culture of their organizations, and on supporting activities and tools.

Institutions face a challenging set of environmental drivers that affect their long-term sustainability and survival. While senior university leaders are vitally occupied with the implications of global competition, fundamental redrawing of funding regimes and associated political contracts with the wider society, and changing expectations of many stakeholders, they are sometimes troubled by the extent of denial that they perceive in their workforces. In a large national programme designed to bring about a 'step change' in the strategic use of learning technologies in higher education, here are some examples identified by institutional leads (typically Pro Vice-Chancellors or Directors of Learning and Teaching) of the challenges they face in leading strategic initiatives concerning learning and teaching:

- '[Lack of awareness of the message] "wake up, innovate, teach better, or perish", with associated mechanisms to help people up their skills'
- 'Resistance of staff, particularly academic staff, to using technology'
- 'Keeping up and being nimble . . . Staff keeping up with students' knowledge'
- 'there are pockets of really poor practice, including poor teaching . . . The inability by some staff members to even realise that they need urgent development in this area is astonishing . . . the challenges I have mentioned here . . . are current ones but also seem to be challenges that will continue into the future, at the cost of all of us in the sector.'. (Leadership Foundation, 2013)

In the face of current realities, there is clearly a wish on the part of senior managers to invoke a stronger sense of 'all being in this together'. There are arguably several factors that undermine this, not least significant of which is the increase in the differentials between mean pay in the higher education sector and salaries for managers in the top tiers.

Research on leadership in universities is often focused on the work undertaken by individual leaders, and resultant extrapolations are made as to the qualities and characteristics required for individual leaders to be successful. In many institutions, these expectations are interpreted and communicated corporately through behavioural competency frameworks. In some cases, these provide examples of illustrative behaviours that exemplify particular competences in use. Sometimes these are accompanied by counter-indicators, which can act as a means to bring into the open ways of working that have hitherto been undiscussible.

In some accounts, the success stories of individual universities are told through the heroic actions of their top leaders. This plays into the hands of what Western (2008) calls the 'Messiah' discourse in which expectations are placed on the shoulders of charismatic individuals to 'save' organizations miraculously.

It is rare to find research that identifies the collective requirements of an organization to be effective. Nevertheless, there is growing evidence that senior leaders understand the importance of such effectiveness. As the outcome of a series of interviews carried out with a range of senior managers from diverse institutions in the UK, Tysome (2013: 18–19) identifies the following characteristics of a successfully led institution. It will:

- clearly identify and communicate its mission and values and define its distinctive position in the HE market – the way it is led and managed and its practices and processes will be built around these;
- introduce flexible practices and processes and employment contracts, by persuading staff of the benefits for their careers and working conditions as well as for the institution;
- be highly focused on students' needs and expectations, but at the same time manage this in such a way as to protect academics from unrealistic demands;
- be run in a more businesslike fashion without being diverted from, or allowing its staff to be distracted from, the core purposes of an HE institution;
- embrace collaboration and provide staff with opportunities to develop by learning from and experiencing different practices and processes from across the sector and from outside HE;
- not allow competition to prevent effective sharing of best practice or the development of mutually beneficial collaborations and partnerships;
- place improving equality and diversity high on its agenda, and have clear, measurable and time-limited objectives in place to achieve this;
- develop good, highly motivated middle managers, particularly departmental heads and deans, and an effective process for selecting staff with strong leadership and management qualities to fill these positions;

- have a sufficiently large and high-quality layer of professional staff supporting its leaders and academics, enabling them to focus on their primary roles and tasks;
- be outward-facing, closely engaging with local, national and international organizations and institutions;
- develop an innovative culture that encourages staff to 'think outside the box' and adopt a proactive response to change;
- introduce and develop performance management in a way that is designed to help staff develop and realize their full potential, rather than focusing on penalizing those that underperform;
- achieve a balance between expecting greater accountability from staff and respecting and supporting academic autonomy;
- ensure that staff, and its senior managers in particular, are well informed of developments that affect the sector, the future of the institution, and the way it is run. It will use this knowledge to respond quickly to emerging opportunities and threats.

Each of these 14 characteristics raises fascinating questions as to how to design and implement the sorts of organizational cultures that would enable them to flourish. The first one alone offers profound opportunities and challenges in a world where institutional missions have been articulated largely in terms of excellence of teaching, research and scholarship – each indistinguishable from the next. Or, as John Burke, my colleague from Jisc, puts it in his ineffable broad Lancashire accent, 'Eh – they were all written by t'same bloke, weren't they?'

Of course, an institution can only 'behave' in a collaborative and constructive manner if its members recognize, value and develop behaviours that support these characteristics. It is all too easy to create 'feel-good' events that inculcate the illusion of working together collectively and cohesively, only to slip back into ingrained patterns of behaviour once the events are over. 'Awayday Syndrome' will be familiar to many readers. The real challenge lies in embedding processes and ways of interrelating that are authentic and are lived out consistently in such a manner that they engender trust. Once trust is in place, many benefits will flow.

This requires a shared and mature sense of leadership identity – not leader identity, where leaders use self-awareness as a means to securing individual benefits, but rather an identity that is profoundly social, and has at its heart a sense of the interdependence of each member of a community with all others. Working towards realizing such a sense of identity, it is entirely possible to perceive everyone as having a leadership role to play. This identifies leadership not as being hierarchical, but as omnipresent. All very well as an idealized state, but where and how do leaders set out on the journey? Chapter 3 begins to set out some practical approaches.

Implications for leadership development

While it may be entirely feasible to identify a set of leadership competences that are required in a given role in an institution of higher education, it is notoriously difficult to measure the extent to which leadership development activities contribute to improvements in such competences. Reasons cited usually focus on the wide range of contextual variables that affect the behaviour of leaders, but there are other barriers to measurement. These might include the discomfort experienced by leaders on their return from developmental programmes, reluctant to practise new approaches in case they are accused of 'going on a management course'.

There might be equal discomfort about seeking feedback from colleagues on changes in behaviour in response to learning from 360-degree surveys based on how those in the workplace perceive them. Furthermore, if the leader's institution has no explicit processes for following up on gauging the return on investment for the expenditure it has committed, the leader is likely to feel not only unsupported; she may feel that nobody in the institution really cares about changes in her leadership approach, that the leadership development experience was enjoyable and possibly offered as a reward for previous good performance, but that ultimately nobody is holding her responsible for any eventual outcomes. As a result of all these factors acting in combination, outcomes may unsurprisingly not transpire.

Lumby points out some salutary lessons from a review of literature on leadership in higher education, notably that 'we do not know how important leadership is; only that people believe it to be so' (2012: 12). She goes on to identify needs for research in particular areas:

> more extensive in-depth evidence about the impact of leadership on teaching and learning, research and enterprise, that is, whether and to what extent outcomes are influenced by leadership . . . Second, we need to fill in some of the gaps about how leaders actually operate, through observation and ethnographic material.
>
> (2012: 13)

Tourish (2012) takes steps to address a gap in the literature by proposing an approach to measuring the impact of leadership development. This involves a clear relationship between the institution and the leaders it seeks to develop. Importantly, the approach is highly contextualized in being linked to the vision and strategy of the institution, and the extent to which these are driven by internal and external environmental factors.

Once the institution has identified change that it wishes to implement, it goes through a process of identifying leadership behaviours appropriate to realizing the change required. The next step is to select people with high potential for strengthening the necessary leadership behaviours, and then to commission interventions that support their development. This is a fascinating approach, which contrasts with that of identifying people to take part in leadership development programmes by virtue of their positional role, or of a range of generic abilities that indicate broad suitability for present or future leadership roles.

The most interesting aspect of Tourish's idea is that the tailored leadership development that he suggests should be commissioned is based on identifying the problems or barriers that might get in the way of the desired change being achieved. These obstructions then become the central focus or content of the developmental challenge. Participating leaders are set the task of solving the problems that have been identified, and provided with appropriate support to aid this. Through processes of reflection, deep learning should then occur which is likely to transfer into practice in the workplace.

In order to measure the extent of the learning that transpires, Tourish proposes a range of indicators:

- behaviour change as perceived by others, measurable through feedback mechanisms which might include 360-degree assessments;
- impact on the institution's performance, in terms of relevant measures related to the change initiative (for instance, student retention, carbon reduction, staff turnover);
- the extent to which the problems identified have been resolved and goals achieved;
- the return (linked to the indicators above) on financial investment.

Learning that results for the institution can then be used to inform future strategy, and so the cycle begins again.

Applying this approach to the design of programmes such as those offered by the Leadership Foundation for Higher Education suggests greater potential than has hitherto been realized for conceiving of the programme as a collaborative venture between a sponsoring university, the individual leader who takes part in the programme, and the team that runs the programme. This clearly implies something quite different from the transactional approach that sometimes characterizes the purchase of a place on a programme. The paying institution is of course likely to have expectations of a transformational experience for the leader who takes part, and these might be voiced from the perspective of a line manager or Human Resources department. The reality, however, is that expectations are only rarely linked to institutional strategy in terms of anything that is communicated to the individual leader, and so huge opportunities are missed.

It would seem to make sense for those designing the leadership development programme to create a more rigorous application process which requires individuals and their institutions to identify the strategic change drivers and demonstrated behaviours that have led to their selection for nomination for the programme. If these behaviours are assessed before and after the programme, rather than at one 'snapshot' point, then a genuine sense of change and progress can be gauged. Finally, perhaps using approaches demonstrated and refined during the programme, all parties concerned might work collaboratively on assessing the impact on the institution and any consequent return on investment. Naturally, achieving all of this requires far deeper evaluation than asking individuals to report on their levels of satisfaction with the programme that they have experienced.

On programmes involving relatively lengthy periods of time and greater resources than, say, a two- or three-day intervention, there is a significant opportunity to experiment with the approach proposed by Tourish. The current manifestation of the Leadership Foundation's flagship Top Management Programme attempts to model this in practice. During the course of the programme, which involves 17 days of direct activity over a six-month period, participants are required to work on leading a specific example of change to which their institution is committed. In regular conversation with their senior institutional sponsor (the Vice-Chancellor, Principal or President of the university), and through constant reflection on the leadership behaviours needed to bring about the change, participants assess the progress they are making. Crucially, and in line with Tourish's thinking, they identify the barriers that make achieving the change become problematic. Facilitated activity on the programme itself then provides appropriate support for individuals as they work in collaboration with peers from other institutions on addressing the identified barriers and obstacles.

The techniques and approaches they use are intended to be transferable into the daily practices of these leaders, and several of them are included as resources in subsequent chapters of this book.

2 Towards the learning organization?

Collective commitment
The benefits of achieving this in our universities

The concept of organizational learning, originating in the 1980s, has proved to be ahead of its time. While it may initially have coexisted with humanistic movements in the history of organizational development – and therefore possibly have been dismissed as a passing fad whose days were numbered whenever recession loomed – it is now turning out to be the bedrock of the kind of collaborative and reflective practices that are so necessary to leading in the complex, interconnected twenty-first-century world.

With its sense of networking, of risk-taking cultures that enable learning to arise from failure, and of the importance of those at the margins of organizations acting as boundary spanners and intelligence gatherers, the idea of the classic learning organization (Pedler et al., 1991; Mabey and Iles, 1989; Senge 1990) is only now beginning to come to fruition in higher education. While systems thinking may have turned out not to do justice to navigating the complexities of our current and future environment, it is worth reflecting that it pre-dated the advent of the internet as a mass medium.

The principles of the learning organization have much to offer higher education institutions. Ironically, given that universities' core business is self-evidently learning, it is difficult to find one that embodies all of the practices called for by these principles. However, increasing numbers are able to evidence progress in at least some of them.

According to the early theorists, learning organizations develop through the learning of individuals and groups working within them, and through an interest in resolving organizational problems through inquiry. Such organizations are able to apply their learning so as to adapt to the changing environment in which they operate, and to contribute through their networks to wider learning in a broader context (often involving partners, suppliers and clients). As such, they are likely to focus clearly on continuous improvement and transformation (Pedler et al., 1991). Implicit in all these characteristics is the notion of collaborative practices.

Tourish supports the importance of working collectively in his identification of a fresh approach to designing and evaluating leadership development:

> The approach outlined here challenges HEIs to utilise a full array of leadership development techniques so that participants are more closely focused on solving problems at work. This is more likely to facilitate a shift from thinking solely about the development of individuals to the development of whole groups or teams as well.
>
> (2012: 19)

There is a fascinating implication here that progress could be made towards universities becoming genuine learning organizations through a focus on intra-institutional approaches to developing leaders collectively. This might work in at least two different ways: firstly, through building cadres of leaders at peer level across institutions and enabling them to become communities of practice of leadership (Wenger, 1998); and secondly, through developing as groups whole teams of individuals who need to work together (such as Faculty or Directorate Management Teams). The latter is most likely to contribute most powerfully towards creating learning organizations, in that if successful it would contribute to building working cultures that would impact directly on organizational practices. The community of practice approach is appealing, and provides a credible peer support network; in practice, nevertheless, there is arguably a greater risk that individuals, once back in their daily working space, would encounter resistance from the prevailing local cultures within their organizational units.

The attractiveness in seeking more overtly to build universities as learning organizations lies in the sense of clear alignment between institutions' approaches to conducting their strategic and operational activities as organizations, and their educational purposes and missions. One way in which one might expect such alignment to manifest itself is in the domain of curriculum design, and its potential contribution to institutional distinctiveness, as seen in the following case study.

CASE STUDY 2: MAASTRICHT UNIVERSITY
An international university with a fully problem-based curriculum

Overview

Maastricht University was founded in 1979 originally to provide an additional medical school and help fill the need for doctors in the local community. Over the past 30 years Maastricht has developed to have over 13,000 students across two campuses:

- the Chemelot Campus
- the Maastricht Life and Science Campus.

The university also has the following divisions for its academic offering:

- Health, Medicine and Life Sciences
- Law
- School of Business and Economics
- Psychology and Neuroscience
- Humanities and Sciences

   o Department of Knowledge Engineering
   o University College Maastricht
   o Maastricht Graduate School of Governance.

Maastricht University (2010)

The university's mission/strategy is:

> Based in Europe, focused on the world. Maastricht University is a stimulating environment. Where research and teaching are complementary. Where innovation is our focus. Where talent can flourish. A truly student-oriented research university.
>
> (www.maastrichtuniversity.nl/web/Main/
> AboutUM/MissionStrategy.htm)

Achievements

In the Times Higher Education World Rankings of 2009, Maastricht University scored 100/100 in the international category, which helped to place it at 116th in the ranking of 40,000 world universities. This achievement, the university believes, is due to:

- developing a vision in the context of what is needed internationally;
- ensuring the institution (and indeed Maastricht itself) is foreigner friendly;
- educating its students for life and not just a qualification;
- deciding that all provision is delivered in English;
- its problem-based learning curriculum.

Problem-based learning

> The Problem-Based Learning system at Maastricht University guarantees a high quality education. Students get more out of their studies, take less time to complete their studies and are overall more satisfied.
>
> (www.maastrichtuniversity.nl/web/Main/ProspectiveStudents/
> Bachelors/OurEducation/CompletionRatesRankings.htm)

Over the 32 years of its existence Maastricht has ensured that all of its provision is in a problem-based learning (PBL) format. It believes it is the only university to do so and that it is this approach to its educational programmes that has enabled it to be effective and efficient. To emphasize this, the institution points out that universities ranked in a similar position to itself have greater funding per student or per academic staff member.

PBL at Maastricht University supports the notion that students are personally responsible for their own academic education and is based on tutorial groups consisting of 14–16 students. The tutor plays a limited part in the discussion during these tutorials but monitors the discussions, provides feedback and where required helps the students to identify relevant problems.

These problems are then researched, debated and discussed by the students to try to derive a solution. It is recognized that in many situations there is not just one answer. By bringing together different views and perspectives, students can derive a common way forward. In working in this way the students realize that no one person, book or technique has all the answers, and learn how to learn effectively together.

'As PBL courses are intensive, students can take only two or three courses at a time depending on the number of credit hours per course' (http:// en.wikipedia.org/wiki/Maastricht_University). The PBL philosophy links with the international agenda of the university as the students learn at their own pace and incorporate their own values, beliefs and cultures. The university's Language Centre offers an introduction to Maastricht's PBL approach for international students.

Questions

1   How efficient and effective is your method of curriculum delivery?
2   Do you view international English-speaking universities as serious competition?
3   How complementary are research and teaching at your institution?

Case study developed by Professor Dawn Forman.

Enablers and barriers
The conditions for organizational learning

One of the macro-environmental factors supporting organizational learning is that of the societal drive towards sharing behaviours. Botsman and Rogers (2011) are leading advocates of collaborative consumption, characterized by patterns of behaviour within a so-called 'sharing economy' that uses technology to disrupt conventional models of doing business. Applied to higher education, Botsman and Rogers's vision implies huge changes to curriculum development, research management, and teaching and learning relationships, *inter alia*.

More immediately, the drivers of research funding point increasingly towards a collaborative approach, particularly in view of the need to work collectively (at departmental and faculty levels) to demonstrate broad impacts of research outputs.

Furthermore, initiatives such as Future Learn, the UK Open University's challenge to United States-dominated propositions such as Coursera, are bringing about greater intra- and inter-institutional collaboration around the need to develop Massive Open Online Courses (MOOCs) – and at an unprecedented pace.

Set in the context of such drivers of change, it is worth considering the critique of thinking about organizational learning by Wang and Ahmed in which they argue that the literature has failed to attend to the importance of 'quantum leap innovation and creativity' (2002: 12) and how these might be enabled in organizations. They outline the enabling attitudes and behaviours that are required in environments characterized by 'hyper-dynamics, uncertainty and chaos' as 'flexibility, proactiveness, innovativeness and energetics' (2002: 13).

There are also numerous behaviours that serve to inhibit the development of learning organizations. Many of these overlap with what has been identified as 'toxic leadership' (Lipman-Blumen, 2005), in which the interests of personal politics dominate institutional discourse. If people communicate guardedly, for fear of humiliation or reprisal, they are unlikely to take risks in bringing new ideas to public fora.

In a toxic, non-learning environment, dialogue is organized so that articulation of innovative proposals can only occur through a set of stilted conventions for communicating and decision-making. This means that people spend inordinate proportions of their working lives in meetings which, while ostensibly driven by rationale and by the deployment of reasoned arguments, are in reality controlled through highly political agendas that allow the chairperson and allies to reach the outcomes they desire. When nearly everyone appears to be complicit in reinforcing the behaviours that characterize this toxic environment, it can be difficult to recognize it for what it is – people effectively become conditioned to behave in set patterns. The toxicity of such an environment derives from the lack of trust that prevails, and the extent to which people feel they have to resort to covert or subversive practices in order to circumvent the system and get things done – assuming, of course, that they have not given up trying to achieve anything within a culture that is so inimical to engagement.

Further barriers to organizational learning include relationships and behaviours that are essentially deferential in nature (see Chapter 4), working within tightly defined organizational boundaries which lead to a 'silo' mentality, and being driven by short-term operational targets. As the architects of organizational culture, leaders are potentially well positioned to redesign in areas where they have influence, and rising to the challenges this poses will be the focus of the rest of this book.

At the Leadership Foundation for Higher Education, we have sometimes found that assumptions made about the impact that can be achieved from commissioning leadership development programmes have actually constrained effective organizational learning. If institutions expect a 'magic bullet' effect from a commissioned programme, they may not be acknowledging their own responsibility for supporting programme participants to maximize their learning. Tourish is clear about the opportunities which come from institutions embracing organizational learning more holistically:

> Formal programmes do make a positive difference. They provide information, challenge outmoded habits, offer fresh perspectives and facilitate networking. But when supplemented by mentoring, coaching, job assignments, job rotation and other interventions designed to sustain deep reflection and ongoing learning in the real world of work, a greater long-term impact can be achieved.

> There is significant evidence that the best forms of leadership development create opportunities for people to learn from their experiences, and then apply what they have learned to solving real and pressing problems in their own organisations. Leadership development activities should therefore focus people's attention on problems they face at work which are likely to impede the achievement of key organisational goals, draw out appropriate lessons and equip them to make a real difference on their return.

> Formal programmes can be supplemented by mentoring, coaching and other interventions designed to sustain deep reflection and ongoing learning in the real world of work. This puts action at the heart of the learning process.
> (2012: 18)

CASE STUDY 3: EMORY UNIVERSITY, ATLANTA, GEORGIA, USA
Developing a learning organization through transformational leadership development programmes

Background

Emory University has for the past three years been nominated for an elite award of the Chief Learning Officers' magazine for its development of a learning organization. This award is given to organizations that establish a learning culture. Emory University is the only academic institution to be shortlisted for such an award, and it has achieved this in each of the three years that it has been available.

This has been achieved through the integrated nature of its Leadership Development Programmes which are championed by the executive vice-presidents within the university. This support has enabled over 900 staff within the organization to have experienced a leadership programme, and such is the commitment to this development that, even at a time of reduced funding, funding has been made available to ensure that these programmes can be maintained.

The Executive Leadership Programmes

Emory University supports three Executive Leadership Programmes. These are:

- the Woodruff Leadership Academy, which is for the health service provision of the university;
- the Academic Leadership Programme, which is primarily for faculty staff;
- the Excellence through Leadership Programme, which is for administrative staff.

Each of these programmes has been developed specifically for the participants it attracts. The programmes are available for staff to apply for, and there are always more people who apply than the programmes can accommodate. Sponsorship by their line manager must accompany each application, and a selection process is conducted to ensure that the appropriate mix of individuals is on each programme and that the individual will gain from the leadership provision. Themes that underpin each of the programmes are:

- a strong emphasis on the individual understanding the strategic priorities and the context in which the university is working;
- networking across the university and understanding how each department and faculty contributes to the strategic goals of the university – it should be noted that Emory is a very diverse university and therefore this aspect is critically important in the development;
- the culture and values of the organization are endorsed and owned by the individuals;
- the programmes aid retention of key staff within the organization.

Around a third of the programmes are common but the emphasis is different in each of the three executive programmes. It is felt helpful to emphasize the differences that each of the programmes provides.

Following successful completion of the programmes, alumni programmes exist to ensure that cross-fertilization provision is made available between the academic support and the faculty leaders. Included within the programmes are different teaching and learning methodologies, including taught provision, action learning projects, coaching provision from external coaches for each of the individuals, a 360 review and use of the Birkman Method to establish the individual's style. Each individual will develop a personal development plan. They will be involved in a team project which will be presented to the university council; four hours' coaching is provided to ensure that the team is ready for the presentation and for the question and answer session at the end of their presentation.

Key outcomes which have been achieved in the organization

1   One project that was developed as a result of a team working on an executive project was a business process review to establish leadership programmes at all levels of the organization. This resulted in a framework for management development programmes being implemented across the university and the establishment of a director for learning and organizational development to ensure this provision could be developed and maintained. A suite of programmes therefore exists for all staff at all levels across the organization and this has been seen as key in enabling the organization to achieve its reputation as a learning organization.

2   Sustainability: Another project that was developed as part of the executive leadership programme looked at sustainability and led to many awards being achieved within the university for environmental sustainability approaches within the organization. The office of sustainability has been established as a direct result of the project outcomes of the executive leadership programme.

3   Parking and transportation: A further project that was reviewed by an executive leadership programme was that of parking and transportation. This has resulted in changes within the bus system to facilitate access to the university, cycle lanes being provided throughout the campus, a bike hire programme, and a zip car programme so that cars are available on campus to ensure that should a member of staff need a car during the day they can acquire one, but they do not need a car to actually come into the university.

Conclusion

The Chief Learning Officers' magazine, *Learning Elite Awards*, reviews each organization against five criteria to establish whether they are a learning organization. Emory University has been selected from over 300 applicants in each of the past three years when the award has been made available. It is the only university in the USA to have been selected for such an award.

Emory University is fully committed to its leadership development provision and has ensured that funding is ring-fenced even in a difficult economic climate so that these leadership development programmes can still take place.

Questions

1   To what extent would you consider your institution to be a learning organization?

2 How does your institution ensure the priorities of its leaders match the strategic goals of the organization?

Case study developed by Wanda J. Hayes, PhD, Senior Director of Learning and Organizational Development, Emory University, Atlanta, and Professor Dawn Forman.

CASE STUDY 4: UNIVERSITY OF MASSACHUSETTS, USA
Transformational change through clear leadership

In 2013, the *Times* of London ranked the University of Massachusetts system 42 among the top 200 universities internationally and 19 for academic reputation and research. UMass Lowell is ranked among the top 100 public universities in the United States, with over 16,000 students and 120 undergraduate, 39 master's and 33 doctoral programmes, and a faculty-student ratio of 17:1. The University has an entrepreneurial approach to all aspects of management of the institution. UMass Lowell's annual fundraising grew 88% in four years. Forbes recently ranked the university 10 on its list of Best Value Colleges in America.

(UMass Lowell at a Glance, 2013)

Background

The University of Massachusetts Lowell appointed a new Chancellor, Marty Meehan, in 2007. At the time of Chancellor Meehan's appointment, the university had had a period of consolidation and almost stagnation; student enrolment was on the decline, the institution had a $5m structural deficit, and, as a consequence, its rating in comparison to other universities in the US was not high. Since the appointment of the new Chancellor, enrolment has increased by 63% and the average SAT score increased by 51 points. The university was ranked for the first time as a top-tier university in 2010 and increased its status in the national US News & World Report rankings by 25 points over the past two years to no. 150. There was a turnaround in the financial profile of the university and during the 2012–13 academic year, six new buildings were completed on the campus. Two more will open within the next few years. This transformation in a seven-year period and against a poor economic climate seems astounding, and therefore it is worth considering the key aspects of change that have been brought about to ensure the university is in a position to capitalize on its current developments and look forward to the future.

The University of Massachusetts Lowell regards itself as a 'Public Entrepreneurial University'. Its strap line is that it provides learning with a purpose to ensure that students are 'work-ready, life-ready and world-ready'. Key changes have been made over the past six years, starting within a month of Marty Meehan taking up his post, in that the whole of the executive team changed within that first month. Key to the appointment of new staff, from within the university and from the local community as well as nationally and internationally, was to select leaders who shared the drive and the passion necessary to ensure that the institution would develop along the lines of the Chancellor's vision.

The institution recruited 'thought leaders' and those who had high expectations both of themselves and of the institution. The Chancellor sought out people who were entrepreneurs, team players, had no egos, had a drive for excellence and were prepared to take risks. One of those individuals is a co-author of this case study, Jacqueline Moloney, who had worked for the institution for 25 years and developed an online provision of $38m. Jacqueline now serves as Executive Vice-Chancellor and is the most senior executive, second only to the Chancellor of the university.

Marty (as he is affectionately called by students, faculty and staff) exhibits the characteristics that he looks for in others, and this is demonstrated in every aspect of his working life – within an office environment, speaking publicly, walking around the campus or participating in keep-fit activities in the university's gym. Marty is described as a considered risk-taker, someone who listens very carefully, makes decisions in a collective and collaborative manner with his team and owns any decision that is taken.

Key mechanisms to ensure continuous improvement and success

The university initiated a comprehensive strategic planning process in 2008 after the Chancellor had been in his post for a year and the majority of senior leaders who make up his executive team were in place. The strategic planning process within the organization is owned by everyone, including students, faculty, staff and other key stakeholders.

More than 200 people actively participated in the development of the current strategic plan – UMass Lowell 2020. Committees were convened to develop plans for what were identified as the university's most urgent challenges and strategic opportunities. The committees were made up of employees and stakeholders from all levels and corners of the university. Considerable benchmarking, research and data development were undertaken to ensure that the priorities of the university and the strategic plan itself were built on firm foundations. As a result, all strategic planning priorities are owned by all faculty, staff and students within the university and are monitored on a regular basis, using a report card mechanism. There is a comprehensive articulation of the institution's key performance indicators (KPIs), and each KPI has a clear individual or group responsible to ensure the targets are reached. While ongoing monitoring occurs, twice-yearly reports on the strategic planning KPIs are reviewed and reported. All information is transparent and shared broadly. Key faculty and staff are made accountable and hold themselves as owners to this accountability.

Overall, through the strategic planning process, and this period of significant change – in fact transformation – the university has managed to gain the trust of all staff with regard to its decision-making process. Interestingly, while the institution has been entrepreneurial in its vision and has taken considerable risks, each decision has been carefully considered and determined to align with the overall vision that the university is trying to achieve. As a result, the university has been successful in its endeavours and has managed to avoid errors in its high-stakes decision-making.

How has this transformation been afforded?

From the outset, the university adopted a set of guiding principles to inform the strategic plan that included striving for excellence, staying focused on the core mission, creating efficiencies and high performance in all aspects of the university, and creating a culture of engagement, innovation and entrepreneurship. During the past seven years the United States, like many other countries, experienced economic challenges which meant that financing has been more difficult to acquire. Key to the success of the institution, therefore, was early bold administrative actions that the new Chancellor drove on his arrival and that included the elimination all non-essential activities in both operations and staff. This resulted in savings of $6.5m on staff costs and $3m in operational efficiency savings. These savings were immediately reinvested in identified strategic initiatives aimed at increasing new streams of revenue.

Admissions and gaining student satisfaction

One of the first changes made was within the admission process, which was rebuilt in the first year, ensuring that a clear journey was articulated from the initial enquiry through to enrolment, induction and retention in the university's programmes. A very strong student-centred focus operates within the university, with monthly meetings being held with student representatives and university leaders. Initially students were intimidated by the interest the Chancellor was showing in their ideas and activities. Now, however, the students are very open, honest and direct with regard to how they report what they feel is right and what needs improvement within the university. The students therefore actively own the decisions that are taken within the university and support changes taking place. One example of this is the students' support for the university's Division I hockey team.

The success of the team is owned not only by the players but by the supporters. In past years, attendance at hockey games was low, averaging around 500 per game. The number of people attending these games today has increased to around 6,000–7,000 on a regular basis, with new records set in the 2013–14 season.

Buying a hotel to aid student accommodation

The university has also supported the students by upgrading their accommodations. The university is expanding the number and variety of residential options for students. More than 1,000 residence hall accommodations have been added recently and the university acquired a hotel in the city centre, which emphasizes its role as part of the city in terms of its profile. An example of the speed with which the institution is able to make decisions, owing to its thoroughness in researching the enterprise before it undertakes it, is that the hotel was acquired and renovated within a 30-day period. Approximately 500 students reside at the hotel, and the remaining hotel facilities operate as an inn and conference centre, generating revenues for the university. This acquisition and residential housing plan were seen by many as a bold initiative, as the hotel was failing as a business prior to the university taking it over.

Review of all aspects of the university processes and establishing the culture

All aspects of the university's work have been reviewed, including all employment policies and practices, service level agreements, and all aspects of research, teaching and learning. This has been achieved through the commitment of key executive leaders and the faculty and staff within the institution.

As one walks round the institution as a visitor, one is struck by the energy level and smiling exchanges with which one is greeted. Such is the culture and community spirit that have been gained. This culture is key to ensuring that the development of the university over the past seven years is sustainable for the future.

Division I aspiration

Another example of the university's development is its aspiration to become a Division I participant for sport. Elevating to Division I in sport was identified as an important initiative in the strategic planning process, but the university did not pursue Division I immediately. It recognized the importance of developing other foundational academic and administrative programmes and services first. Faculty-generated new undergraduate, master's and doctoral-level programmes were established, and the research profile was increased. Up to 50 members of faculty and staff were involved in the decision-making process. Student experience was seen as key to the development. Considerable research and reviews were undertaken to ensure this aspiration would be achievable. The institution's aim to be a Division I player in the sports arena was realized when it accepted the invitation in February 2013 to join a Division I conference, America East. Like UMass Lowell, America East values academic achievement highly and the conference has the third-highest average GPA among all Division I conferences in the country.

Concluding remarks

The University of Massachusetts Lowell regards itself as having an entrepreneurial spirit, which is evident in the commitment of the faculty and staff to this leadership approach. It believes this spirit will be evident in all graduates who complete programmes at the institution in the future. To help ensure that it graduates entrepreneurial-spirited students, the university has launched an annual $25,000 Difference Maker innovation competition, in which 45 teams of four to five students participate. It will be interesting to review the University of Massachusetts Lowell's development in another seven years.

Questions

1   In your view, how distinctive is the concept of the 'public entrepreneurial university'?
2   How effective were the mechanisms deployed by the university to ensure continuous improvement and success?
3   In what circumstances do you think it is appropriate for a university to diversify into running additional businesses such as hotels?

Case study developed by Jacqueline Moloney, Executive Vice Chancellor, University of Massachusetts Lowell; Lauren Turner, Associate Vice Chancellor for Human Resources and Equal Opportunities and Outreach, University of Massachusetts Lowell; and Professor Dawn Forman.

These case studies provide rich examples of the approaches to organizational learning being taken in different institutions, and demonstrate the impact that leading strategically can make. In the rest of this book, we shall identify specific practices that can be deployed by leaders at all levels in universities in order to bring about change effectively, and to engender organizational learning.

3 Catalysts for collaborative working

Learning conversations

In order to sustain themselves, it could be argued that universities must attract, develop and retain those with the greatest leadership potential, at all levels of their organizations. In order to achieve the highest levels of collaborative working, leadership should ideally be widely distributed across many layers of institutional departments, and across institutions. Through applying 'deep' approaches to organizational learning, it is possible to develop *strategic capabilities* which are at the roots of long-term organizational sustainability (NCSL, 2005a). These are:

- understanding learning and its impact on students and staff
- manifesting a culture of trust, communication, creativity and innovation
- nurturing a reflective community
- applying positive team approaches to problem-solving.

Sustainable universities are likely to take opportunities to use existing processes of planning and consultation to undertake dialogue internally and externally and to build links with their communities, and professionals working in them are able to articulate clearly what they would like their organizations to look like in the future.

NCSL (2005a) has found that *strategic conversations* are vital. These are about negotiating an agreed language to help practitioners examine what they do. Specifically, this language enables participants to:

- learn about each other's work
- build collaborative capabilities
- learn how to enquire
- learn how to reflect
- learn how to bring about action related to desired change
- learn how to evaluate each other's work and its impact.

This book places considerable emphasis on developing the *facilitation and evaluation* capacities needed at all levels within institutions in order to bring about sustainable change that is widely owned by participating professionals.

This chapter will draw eclectically on theories of cultural learning (e.g. social constructivist, reflective practice, situated learning, learning communities) in order to design approaches to collaboration in which learning is seen as participation, and where 'knowledge embedded in the members can be shared if there is mutual engagement, joint enterprise, a shared repertoire and negotiation of meaning in practice . . . Not enough emphasis is placed on informal learning' (NCSL, 2005b: 15).

Situated learning emphasizes the importance of collaborative, constructive learning taking place in real situations. This implies that learning activities should allow for the application of cycles of experiential learning, in which reflection, abstraction and generalization are key to the ability to change professional practice.

Leaders who are skilled in facilitation scaffold the learning process for participants in learning conversations, thus providing the social context in which learning occurs, according to the social constructivist perspective.

Wenger emphasizes that traditional approaches to learning, with their focus on individual performance, do not favour collaboration, and therefore hinder the emergence of what he calls *communities of practice*, promoting 'learning in the context of the lived experience of participation in the world' (1998: 3). For Wenger, learning derives from meaning, practice and community, and it gains strength when learners become more aware of the discourse they use when discussing their own practice. This learning discourse is based on mutual engagement, of which the key characteristics are as follows.

- *Joint accountability:* the community agrees, and reinforces through continuous review and reflection, a set of ground rules governing expected patterns of behaviour and language.
- *Negotiation:* the ground rules may need revising in light of practice, and are seen by the community as being open to renegotiation as appropriate.
- *Engagement with diversity:* for any community to be authentically inclusive, its leaders must ensure that they model good practice in equality and diversity. This entails full recognition of the range of gender, ethnicity, sexuality, disability and other differences found within the community of practice. It is crucial also to be mindful of the extent to which the community of practice excludes, whether intentionally or not, those who are not acknowledged as belonging.
- *Shared responsibility for maintaining the community of practice:* there is no sense of hierarchy governing who should take the initiative, which resides with every individual member.

Successful participation in the community 'is recognisable as competence', according to Wenger. Facilitators of learning conversations therefore need to be equipped to help professionals develop appropriate competence in participation, and to be attentive to the indicators that communities of practice are forming.

In terms of impact, Wenger stresses the importance of those who are the direct beneficiaries of the educational system, our students: 'we must become reflective with regard to our own discourses of learning and to their effects on the ways we design for learning' (1998: 8–9).

This chapter sets out some examples of processes through which it is possible to identify and develop the learning that derives from informal dialogue between practitioners, with a view to making it explicit and consciously self-aware as a *learning conversation*.

It is argued that leaders who engage are likely to display and model particular characteristics, including personal and professional networking and high-quality personal and interpersonal skills that apply emotional intelligence (Goleman, 1995). The basis for developing these skills and characteristics is to build on self-understanding of management and communication styles, strengths and areas for development in order to create and nurture working environments in which genuine collaboration is seen as a desired norm. The use of personal behaviour profiling forms an important catalyst for individual and team-based change.

ILERN (2007) defines three types of leadership that are not mutually exclusive: all overlap, but with distinctive characteristics.

- *Democratic leadership*, concerned with social justice, empowerment and developing critical understanding of power interests.
- *Facilitative leadership*, in which all members of an organization are seen as learners, the potential of individuals is developed, and task-orientation is focused on problem-solving.
- *Distributed leadership*, where sharing of responsibility for decision-making is devolved to all levels of an organization, and all members are perceived as being – to some extent – leaders.

The prevailing understanding of leadership that exists in a community of professionals has a significant bearing on the way in which members of that community behave, and is likely itself to prove a worthwhile topic of reflection and analysis.

Action learning

This chapter focuses on tools for building professional dialogue. Of particular help in this is action learning. This has been identified as powerful, as it:

- develops and enhances reflective practice
- catalyses teamworking
- facilitates collective leadership capacity
- enables distributed leadership

- wins commitment from participants to wider organizational change and learning
- sustains organizational capability and culture. (Gentle, 2010)

Simple ground rules are established prior to the first meeting, including:

- confidentiality within the group
- open sharing of information
- active and respectful listening
- sensitivity to others' contexts and circumstances
- willingness to be challenged
- ownership by individuals of actions relevant to their issue
- avoidance of judgemental statements
- commitment to remaining on-task
- respect for the process and equal allocation of time between participants
- commitment to generating options for action, rather than prescriptive solutions.

Topics or issues for action learning sets

Selection of a participant's topic should be based on an issue that is likely to evolve over the next three to six months, and that lends itself to regular 'revisiting' in the set's discussions.

Occasionally, circumstances will arise for an individual during the life of an action learning set that have over time become more pressing than the topic they originally proposed. In this case it may be more helpful to move the focus to the new issue. Indeed, it is hoped that actions generated through the set will assist earlier resolution or progress of issues and challenges.

RESOURCE 2: HOW IS AN ACTION LEARNING SET RUN?

It is not usually realistic to set aside more than half a day for an action learning set session – this model shows how time might be used for a set with six members (one facilitator, five presenters).

1 Set opening (five minutes)
2 Presentation and analysis of issues (30 minutes per presenter)
3 Drafting and suggestion of action plans (20 minutes)
4 Review of the process of the set meeting handled as a round (five minutes).

At the start of their respective 30-minute time slot, each presenter takes a maximum of three minutes to outline their own project, ending with a key question about an issue they would like to learn more from: how to overcome a barrier, how to understand underlying reasons, etc.

The remaining time in the slot is used for challenging and clarifying questions, all within an atmosphere of trust, confidentiality and support. Other participants resist the temptation to make suggestions. Ideas for action to be worked on by each presenter/problem-owner are put forward during Stage 3, at the end of the session.

The collaborative learning that the participants experience is usually very different from other forms of dialogue with which they might be more familiar – the effect can be powerful.

What actually happens in an action learning set? When introducing action learning, a group may feel some initial discomfort with a process that can seem stilted. This can lead to set members feeling self-conscious, and occasionally the facilitator may need to respond to comments which suggest that the process involves 'navel-gazing' or 'group therapy'. Such remarks often stem from defensiveness, and usually abate once set members grasp the purpose and practices of action learning. The effects of intense listening and questioning that result from a successful set meeting are usually evident, and are felt by set members to be productive.

Nevertheless, it should be stressed that it is helpful at the outset for a set to commit to a series of set meetings at regular intervals (for instance, monthly meetings over a 6-month period), since there is a clear sense that as a group learns over time to support and challenge one another, tangible learning benefits accrue. On more than one occasion, I have heard examples from universities of senior managers who return from leadership development programmes, filled with evangelical zeal about action learning sets, and then seek to impose them on their institutions. Unsurprisingly, they report that 'we tried that once, and it didn't work'. On further investigation, it transpires that there are preconditions for successful action learning that they have not observed. For instance, sets have comprised mixed groups of middle managers, each of which had a senior manager in it, thus inhibiting conversation and raising suspicions that colleagues were being monitored. On other occasions, no rationale was provided for embarking on action learning.

Action learning can be particularly effective when it brings together diverse groupings of managers who do not normally work collaboratively. The lack of detailed knowledge that set members possess of the working contexts in which the other set members are based does not work as a barrier to learning, but instead seems to encourage genuinely open and unconstrained questions. These can lead to real insights for presenters.

This is not to say, however, that action learning cannot work within organizations, or even sub-units of organizations where participants work together regularly. Earlier in my own career, I carried out an experiment within a department in an institution of higher education, and concluded that in such settings there are particular factors that need to be taken into account when introducing action learning.

I reflected on the original 'equation' postulated by the creator of action learning, Reg Revans, in which Learning (L) is the outcome of a combination of Programmed knowledge (P), Questioning (Q) and Reflection (R). Revans (1983) found that action learning sets were effective when they combined the application of technical or management expertise with the capabilities needed to ask powerful questions and to engage in reflection, arguably covering both domains of content and process. The equation is therefore $L = P + Q + R$.

Compared with the territory covered in many meetings in universities, this calls for a sense of organizational maturity that is not always in evidence – but that can be nurtured and developed by leaders.

I found two further variants in the equation – Affective factors (which might be known as A) and the influence of political Conflict (which might be known as C) with the wider organizational values and practice where action learning is situated. The emotional charge that is present in every action learning set session may be broadly positive or negative (or perhaps sometimes neutral), and is likely to vary considerably according to the extent to which the set members feel collectively in or out of favour with the institutional *Zeitgeist*, which in an era of turbulence can shift frequently during the course of an academic year. The formula thus becomes $L = P + Q + R + (A - C)$. Leaders who initiate action learning within their own organization will need to be sensitive to, and know how to adjust to, the emotional and political climate at any given session, if learning – and consequent effective action – is to result (Gentle, 2010).

Collaborating for educational impact

Action learning can work effectively in situations where professional colleagues are committed to bringing about changes in the educational experiences offered in universities.

In a mass higher education system that is largely operated through modular curriculum designs, there is a danger that students' experience of learning becomes fragmented and lacking in cohesion. The greater the range of flexibility and choice, the higher is the risk that graduates receiving a named degree award actually demonstrate a diffused set of attributes which scarcely enhance the reputation of the qualification or its awarding institution.

A number of universities are addressing this potential risk by moving away from modular designs, and 'reinventing' course structures. Liverpool Hope University is one such case, and the lessons learned to date in terms of organizational culture and learning are fascinating.

Liverpool Hope has moved beyond a fragmentation of learning (often associated with a modular curriculum structure) to having a rounded formation of the graduate in the discipline. To this end each academic department has developed the notion of a 'disciplinary core' ensuring that all students studying a subject area (whether as single or combined honours) have a commonality of experience and learning, which reflects the concept of the graduate in the discipline. In each subject the curriculum is designed to actively support student progression and enhancement; it is not split into artificial units such as modules, but involves a journey through the discipline that deepens and allows specialism as each student moves through years of study. To achieve this end, staff and students are provided with opportunities for enhanced engagement and deep learning, with the design of provision at all levels encompassing seminars and small group tutorials. The university has made a commitment to each student that they will have tutorials in groups of 10 or fewer with a named tutor each week, that all teaching should be research-informed and that each student will have an experience that is led both by academic teams and by student engagement.

Gibbs et al. (2009) identify the conditions for effective leadership of academic departments in which a central aspiration is to increase the degree of engagement by students and staff in the educational processes that support appropriate learning in a given discipline, or set of disciplines. Having undertaken empirical research across 22 departments in a range of highly ranked research-intensive universities, the authors coded the resultant case studies against four different theoretical frameworks.

Of particular interest here are the frameworks developed by Ramsden (1998), around conceptions of the organization of teaching, and by McBeath et al. (2004) concerning how leadership is distributed.

In both cases, the frameworks imply a progressive spectrum that moves from a limited, control-oriented view towards one that is more expansive, focused more on professional growth, development and process (Gibbs et al., 2009: 36). For instance, in the case of the conceptions of teaching, at one end of the spectrum is 'A focus on the bureaucratic structure and organisation of the department, imposed by the head' (Gibbs et al., 2009: 36). At the opposite end is:

> A focus on teaching emphasizing the students' experience of studying in a continually changing and developing curriculum. How to change and improve is the subject of systematic discussion and consultation and the head systematically establishes means to enable teachers to develop.
>
> (Gibbs et al., 2009: 36)

There is considerable concern around the world over how university leaders give attention to engaging students in the life of institutions. In some cases, this means basic representation on course committees and institutional governing bodies. In others, it may mean that students are actively involved in managing the activities of the institution, particularly those that have a bearing on the curriculum and its educational outcomes.

Gibbs et al.'s suggestions that those departments which emphasize students' experience as effective partners in a co-created learning experience might be considered at the radical or progressive end of a spectrum are worthy of further consideration as to the implications for the practices and behaviours of leaders. Others, too, have proposed scales for defining the extent of partnership working with students. Fielding and Bragg (2003) outline a framework for a set of reciprocal processes in which students engage with research alongside educational professionals, with six increasingly developmental approaches identified:

1 Students as a data source (staff utilize information about student progress and well-being) . . .
2 Students as active respondents (staff invite student dialogue to deepen learning/professional decisions) . . .
3 Students as co-enquirers (staff take the lead role with high-profile, active student support) . . .
4 Students as knowledge creators (students take the lead role with active staff support) . . .
5 Students as joint authors (students and staff decide on a joint course of action) . . .
6 Intergenerational learning as lived democracy (shared commitment to/ responsibility for the common good). (Ward, 2013: 7)

This correlates closely with the Economic and Social Research Council's Teaching and Learning Research Programme, which highlighted a workplace cultural continuum depicting an idealized 'expansive' organizational culture in which growth, support and development thrive (Table 3.1).

In defining educational benefits for students, and factors that contribute to enhancing these benefits, Gibbs (2010) cites the work of Chickering and Gamson (1987). Their seven principles of good pedagogical practice also point to an expansive working environment. A thought process that translates these principles into practices for leaders in higher education raises questions about the extent of alignment between:

(a) the working cultures experienced in universities by their workforces; and
(b) the espoused practices, and underlying values, of the learning and teaching ecosystem.

The seven principles are explored in the following pages.

1 *Good practice encourages staff–management contact*

Frustration is often reported on the part of administrative staff at departmental and faculty level that academics do not prioritize their engagement with these groupings of colleagues. Indeed, to the extent that the work of professional

Table 3.1 Workplace environments and leadership (adapted from Evans et al., 2006)

Restrictive	Expansive	Implications for organizational leadership
Limited interpersonal support	Interpersonal support from more senior project members/members of institution	Leader uses coaching conversations to challenge colleagues constructively, and to promote a distributed approach to leadership in the organization
Limited exposure to multiple communities of practice	Supported engagement with multiple communities of practice	Leader role-models highly effective networking, and takes developmental approach to connecting colleagues to relevant networks
Hierarchical valuing of skills, with privileging of some team members	Multidimensional model of expertise with diverse skills of entire research team valued	Leader encourages open discussion of skills and capabilities of all members of the organization, and recognizes/learns from the value of contributions made by others
Prioritization of project outputs over professional development needs of individuals	Balance between project outputs and researcher's own professional development	Leader ensures that regular planning/review of personal and professional development are seen as important; leader enhances this as a priority by developing internal networking schema
Limited access to off-the-job training	Access and encouragement to attend off-the-job training	As above; leader ensures that sufficient resources are available to meet colleagues' developmental needs
Abrupt ending to the project with no further investment in research staff	Ongoing commitment to researchers' futures beyond the completion of the project	Leader cultivates an organizational culture that values belonging and contributing to mutually beneficial and sustainable futures

services staff can be perceived to be driven by corporate institutional aspirations, this work is sometimes seen as being inimical to concepts of academic freedom and an implied right not to be controlled by so-called managerialism (Bolden et al., 2012).

Leaders who wish to model good practice in bridging such gaps in perception can draw on some of the activities outlined in this section.

RESOURCE 3: BUILDING SUCCESSFUL TEAM WORKING AROUND A COMMON PURPOSE

This workshop is designed to enhance a sense of team working among colleagues, and is easy for a leader (such as a Head of Department, Director or Dean of Faculty) to set up. It works across a broad range of themes – the example given here focuses on team working, but the workshop would work equally well for other important aspects of colleagues' work in the institution, such as a productive research environment, or an engaged student experience.

Stage 1 (10 minutes) – Brainstorm success characteristics

- Set scene and quickly outline the process.
- Encourage participants to spend a moment reflecting on characteristics exhibited by teams when they are working successfully (or any other theme you wish to choose, where success is crucial). How would you recognize success when you see it? Behaviours? (Avoid underlying reasons – these will come in the next stage.)
- Give participants five minutes to write own Post-Its and stick onto flipchart.
- Harvest Post-Its and reorganize on flip – encouraging group to cluster common themes where possible (five minutes).
- Facilitator or participants highlight key themes.

Stage 2 (10 minutes) – Identify and prioritize blockers and enablers

- This is conducted by forming two groups who look at blockers and enablers separately (using flipchart) and then report back to each other.
- Encourage participants to brainstorm ideas in response to the questions – usual rules of brainstorming apply.
- Reorganize what emerges into thematic clusters or groupings.
- Prioritize the groupings in terms of impact (possibly through the use of dot or tick voting or simply by volume).

- Often the same blockers and enablers will appear against different success characteristics.

Stage 3 (20 minutes) – Convert blockers and enablers into positive aims

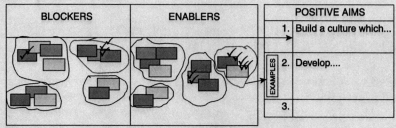

- For the key blockers, the group should generate ideas as to how these can be converted into positive aim statements.
- For enablers, the group should generate a set of positive aims focused on strengthening the impact of each enabler further.
- Ideally, the group should try to generate four or five positive aims.

Stage 4 (five minutes) – Wrap up

- Summarize the journey: quickly reiterate the steps that the group has just gone through (or ask participants to describe them).
- Prompt discussion and thinking as to how outcomes may be applied.

Example questions that could be posed:

- Do you think that this was a good group to conduct this exercise?
- How might different groups of people be involved in this type of exercise?
- Could you see this being something that could be used with students/ employers etc.?
- Would this be something that you could see being used in an Away Day? TDA (2007)

2 Good practice encourages cooperation among staff

On one hand, successfully functioning academic teams appear essential in the context of organizing effective and coherent programmes of learning and teaching. On the other, the measures devised for demonstrating success in research endeavour (particularly the quality of individual published outputs) can often reinforce solitary working. Cooperation between staff seems to vary according to perceptions of the relative value of these core activities of the university. In disciplinary fields where collaboration in research is a greater contributor to successful outcomes, a higher degree of propensity for pedagogical cooperation might be expected.

RESOURCE 4: GENERATING COLLABORATIVE SOLUTIONS

This activity involves drawing on the collective resources and insights of a small group (five to 12 individuals), using a sharp and highly structured session that generates a number of solutions to a problem identified by one person – the Problem Owner.

There are five separate 5-minute stages, as follows.

1   Problem Owner presents the context of the issue, concluding with a 'How can I/how might we . . .?' question (maximum two minutes). Using questions, the rest of the group clarifies more detail on the nature of the problem. There must be no focus on solutions at this stage.

2   Ideas for approaches or alternatives to address the problem are generated as a brainstorm activity and recorded on a flipchart. There should be no discussion or judgement of suggestions. The five minutes should be used to enable a flow of ideas – emphasis on quantity over quality. At the end of the time slot, the Problem Owner should identify the two most useful ideas by circling them – no justification or explanation is needed for the selection.

3   Divide the group into two, allocating one of the circled ideas to each half. Ask the groups to identify benefits and constraints for each idea.

4   The Problem Owner should circle constraints that are critical concerns – i.e. if they were not addressed, the idea could not be realized. These should be explored in discussion to determine whether the idea needs to be modified. If the critical constraints can be overcome, proceed to the final stage. If not, continue by developing one of the other ideas.

5   The Problem Owner suggests an action plan for each idea, using the expertise in the group to shape proposed actions. The facilitator may wish to conclude by inviting feedback from the Problem Owner on the process and outcomes of the activity. (TDA, 2007)

3 Good practice encourages active learning

Learning-centric departments, whether in professional services or academic domains, are likely to achieve better performance outcomes, according to the tenets of learning organization thinking. Setting aside time for learning can prove to be a worthwhile investment if it avoids expensive mistakes being made, or enables better communications. Yet ironically, as seats of learning, universities often seem reluctant to embrace these tenets authentically. In their anxiety to be businesslike, institutions can be tempted to see organizational learning as 'soft' and perhaps over-indulgent, rather than as a set of rigorous processes for improving the quality of outputs, outcomes and impact.

4 Good practice emphasizes time on task

In pedagogical terms, this refers to the allocation of time, often in scheduled classroom sessions, for learning activity that goes beyond receiving transmitted input. The underlying principle is that learning is more profound when the learner is engaged in responding to a challenge that forces questioning and application of the subject matter. The task that is set is intended to enable mental processing of concepts, and at the same time is often designed to have affective appeal – thus engaging both hearts and minds.

On a Center for Creative Leadership (CCL) leadership development programme in which I participated in 2013, and that I found particularly engaging and transformative, I analysed the use of scheduled classroom time in terms of different categories of activity (Figure 3.1), and was struck by the fact that a very small proportion of the total time was spent in plenary sessions. Most of that was taken up by briefing for subsequent group tasks, and in fact under 2 hours was used to present models of leadership in ways that might be described as transmitting programmed knowledge. This was on a week-long programme!

How might this concept of time on task apply then to one of the most common uses of time reported by staff when describing their contribution to

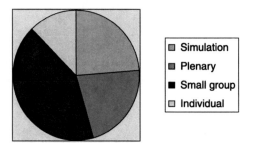

Figure 3.1 Proportional allocation of activity time on CCL's *Leading for Organizational Impact programme*

organizational life – participating in meetings? The word 'participating' is itself contestable. Reflecting on the body language of people during the hundreds, possibly even thousands of meetings you have attended during your career in higher education, how much disengagement have you seen? How does this manifest itself?

There is some anecdotal evidence, reported by participants on leadership development programmes, of conscious attempts by university leaders in recent years to change this picture. Approaches to meetings are explored further in the next chapter.

5   *Good practice communicates high expectations*

Developing shared understandings of expectations is surely a core task of leaders. Buckingham (2007) argues that leadership is fundamentally about 'rallying people towards a better future', and that this can be achieved by constant reinforcement and revisiting of questions that serve to provide clarity. He identifies four key questions around which leaders can develop discourse concerning expectations:

- Who do we serve?
- What is our core strength?
- What is our core success measure?
- What actions can we take today?

Helping individuals to ponder these questions meaningfully can become the stuff of everyday corridor conversations, as well as a useful focus for coaching-style one-to-one and team meetings, and should not be confined to annual performance reviews.

At one stage in my university career, I remember taking pride in the feedback from the colleagues whom I had responsibility to appraise. The institution was attempting to introduce a devolved appraisal system that would have meant that I could reduce my workload by delegating some 30 appraisals to colleagues, and this was resisted by those who felt that they would lose their annual opportunity to have 'quality time' with their Head of Department. At the time I found this flattering. It was only on reflection that I realized the extent to which I had failed to use the myriad opportunities available, day in and day out, to lead high-quality learning conversations with people I was seeking to motivate.

6   *Good practice respects diverse talents and ways of learning*

In a pluralistic society, learning and teaching processes clearly need to reflect the cultural orientations, preferred learning approaches and concerns of class, ethnicity, gender, disability and sexuality that may be represented in any given group of students. Similarly, leaders need to demonstrate equivalent and parallel respect in engaging with those they seek to motivate, and to model the behaviours they expect others to demonstrate.

Recent research on academic leadership (Bolden et al., 2012) also suggests that these principles, if applied for instance to the development and support processes for inducting new researchers, also apply to the research work of universities – and arguably that of knowledge transfer, and of all the central supporting services provided by institutions.

There is an implication here of the importance of harnessing the energy and ideas of all those in an organization, not only those central to power structures. Including those at the margins, who operate across the boundaries of the formal institution and are often the greatest innovators, is critical.

7 Good practice gives prompt feedback

As we will see in Chapter 5, working cultures characterized by constant, constructive feedback between colleagues are relatively rare in higher education. Whether there is a correlation between the widespread absence of such practice among academic staff, and students' perceptions (as voiced repeatedly in National Student Surveys and other such metric instruments) that they are generally less satisfied than in other aspects of universities' provision with the speed and quality of feedback they receive from academics, is debatable.

Professional learning communities

NCSL identifies the challenge of creating, developing and sustaining a 'professional learning community' as a 'major strategic leadership and management task' (2006: 8). The claimed benefits for teaching staff of developing successful professional learning communities are that they enable a collective focus on improving student learning. Professional learning communities are said to enhance collaborative working across a department or school through valuing enquiry and action research in learning and teaching, and through encouraging reflective practice. Furthermore, they promote a working culture in which colleagues learn from and with each other.

A final claim in favour of professional learning communities is that they nurture a climate in which people are open to change, and in which 'risk-taking, creativity and innovative thinking are encouraged' (NCSL, 2006: 2).

Those communities of practice that are successful acquire the capability to track and evaluate their progress over time, learning from setbacks as well as successful achievements. In doing so, they build shared vocabularies for discussing their development and, when mature, display a capacity for interdependence. In

Tuckman's (1965) framework of team development, groups reaching the zenith of collaborative growth display characteristics associated with high performance and self-reliance, such as sharing a common focus, communicating effectively and being able to solve problems. If these are the claims to be made for professional learning communities, how might such high-performance attributes be evaluated?

Tuckman emphasized the overwhelming tendency for teams to focus on the content of what they are trying to achieve or discuss, with a consequent failure to give sufficient attention to process (how teams approach tasks and challenges, and learn from them) or to the affective dimension (how team members feel about their engagement in the team's activities).

It may be helpful to think of the scope of evaluation of the workings of professional learning communities and other teams (however they may prefer to define themselves) in higher education as including the following.

Content

- examining the strategic and operating environment
- visioning and horizon-scanning
- understanding current capabilities and planning to extend these
- market investigation
- planning and implementing change
- assessing priorities to aid decision-making
- outputs and activities of individual members of the community.

Process

- observational and reflective processes
- surveys and diagnoses of organizational climate and/or culture
- assessment of impact of the community's activities
- discursive processes for examining a range of views, arguments and propositions.

Affective domain (see Chapters 4 and 5)

- empathizing with stakeholder experiences
- inquiry into 'emotional signature' of the community's processes and outcomes
- affective impact of the community's own learning activity
- giving, receiving and acting on feedback.

Across these categories, we can draw on detailed sets of tools that can be found below and in subsequent chapters.

RESOURCE 5: EVALUATION MATRIX

Using a flipchart at each table (with three rows and two columns), individuals in table groups write Post-Its in response to three different categories, and paste them on the chart in the left-hand column:

Row 1: What's working well?
Row 2: What's so-so?
Row 3: What's not working well?
(10 minutes)

Groups then generate ideas for what to do in response to the ideas on the flipchart, creating new Post-Its for:

Celebrate success (What's working well?)
Quick wins (What's so-so?)
Key challenges (What's not working well?)
(20 minutes)

Allow groups to circulate to other tables, and open up a plenary discussion on possible options for action. Alternatively, delegate this to three separate groups, each discussing one of the rows and corresponding sets of ideas generated.
(20 minutes)

RESOURCE 6: DIAMOND NINE-CARD SORT ACTIVITY

Make several sets of laminated cards of 12–15 cards each, and give one pack to each group of between six and eight participants. The cards should contain strategic aspiration statements that might be true of the university in two to four years' time (this is an example – though any time scale would work).

Each table group discusses to agree an order for the top three aspirations that they think will make the biggest impact/difference over the next two or three years, then the next six aspirations, arranged in a diamond shape in front of each group. Each table should have a card arrangement that looks like this:

Priority 1

Priority 2   Priority 3

Priority 4   Priority 5   Priority 6

Priority 7   Priority 8

Priority 9

Some cards will be discarded. You may wish to give each group some blank cards for them to write one or two additional aspiration statements of their own.

After 10 minutes, ask each table to report back, noting similarities and differences. There's usually a clear sense of commonality between at least some of the top three across the groups.

RESOURCE 7: STAKEHOLDER VISIONING

Organize the room into table groups, ideally with four to six people on each table. Give a brief outline of the importance of stakeholder management within the strategic planning process. Ask the groups to choose four different categories of stakeholders that have high power and high interest as far as the university is concerned.

Use flipcharts, each one of which has the name of one key stakeholder for the university, and four quadrants, labelled:

Say   Feel

See   Do

Groups spend five minutes on each chart, then rotate so they cover all four, writing Post-Its for 'By July 2017, what do we want X to . . . Say, See, Feel, Do?'

After building up a vision for each stakeholder group, focus discussion for as long as you need on the actions you should take in the short, medium and long terms in order to realize the vision. Remember to allocate clear responsibilities, success criteria and timescales for each action you will need to take.

RESOURCE 8: FURTHER CARD SORT THEMES

These can serve as a fascinating catalyst to conversations that seek to identify the challenges and opportunities in your workplace culture. The first set is intended to stimulate discussion about perceived behaviours as manifested across an institution (Table 3.2). The second set is intended to be helpful for discussion on priorities or capabilities within a university school or department (Table 3.3).

Table 3.2 Set of card sort themes: perceived behaviours

Leadership is seen as part of every professional job role at the university	Collaboration is a core skill of all university staff	Learning from other institutions and other sectors is endemic in the university's culture
Communication and feedback across all layers of the university are improving constantly	The entire organization is focused on the future direction of the university	People at the university are enabled to be leaders without necessarily having a formal management role
Academic staff are good citizens of the university, with a clear service orientation	Professional services staff are more strongly focused on outcomes than on processes	Leaders are good at fostering high performance, and are passionate about achieving results for the university
Leaders encourage others to identify and pursue their own development needs in pursuit of organizational improvement	The university's leaders demonstrate curiosity and innovation and are prepared to take appropriate risks (and make decisions and stick to them)	The university's leaders challenge assumptions and are creative around problems and solutions
The university nurtures our people by coaching that recognizes the strengths of the individual and the team	The university's leaders recognize the impact of their behaviour on students and colleagues	The university is committed to enabling front-line staff to contribute to innovative solutions

Table 3.3 Set of card sort themes: priorities and capabilities

Delivering on commitments	Finding the energy and drive to inspire others to follow	Developing a strategic plan for the school
Developing staff reporting to the Head of School	Being resilient in standing by decisions and seeing them enacted	Managing people and the complex personal agendas that motivate them
Developing and maintaining active networks	Playing an active role as a member of Faculty Board in developing strategy	Delivering the strategic plan for the school
Complying with legislation and university policies, including health, safety and the environment	Monitoring the progress of the school against agreed objectives and targets	Being efficient and effective in managing finances and resources
Developing specific school strategies (research and knowledge transfer, teaching and learning)	Taking cabinet responsibility for decisions taken by the Faculty Board	Ensuring efficient management and operation of taught programmes

RESOURCE 9: PROGRESS CHART

Monitoring is only useful when it is followed up with action.

Here are two complementary approaches to **considering actions you have taken** at different stages in the progress of your project, or in the development of your professional learning community. They are designed to aid reflection and to focus planning for what to do next.

Approach A

Think about the broad phase you have reached in your journey, what has helped you and what has held up progress. What phase have you now reached? (See Table 3.4.)

Approach B

A reflective timeline allows you to think back periodically over the work that you have done to consider the actions that you took at different stages and, in retrospect, to reflect on their value in helping to develop the professional learning community.

Think back over what you have done and create a reflective timeline. Figure 3.2 shows a sample timeline, with some examples of peaks and troughs in the experience of the professional learning community. You will need to create your own timeline, with approximate dates and highlighting ebbs and flows, and reasons for these, in the appropriate places.

Table 3.4 Summary of phases (NCSL, 2006)

	Starting out *Acquiring information and beginning to use ideas*	Developing *Experimenting with strategies and building on initial commitment*	Deepening *Well on the way, having achieved a degree of mastery and feeling the benefits*	Sustaining *Introducing new developments, and re-evaluating quality – Professional Learning Community as a way of life*
When, approximately, did this happen?				
What were the most valuable processes in helping you to reach this phase?				
Which things didn't work, and why?				
What might you do next?				

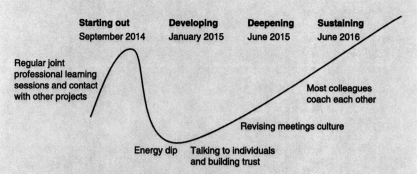

Figure 3.2 Reflective timeline

Questions for reflection and dialogue

Which were the most successful strategies and actions? Why? Did the timing when they were carried out have anything to do with their success?

Which were the least successful strategies and actions? Why? Did the timing of when they were undertaken have anything to do with their lack of success?

Were there any internal or external factors that hindered the team's development as a professional learning community? If yes: what were these? Were they overcome successfully or not?

How can you build on the process?

If you were advising or supporting colleagues in other teams starting on the journey, what might you suggest they do?

RESOURCE 10: PRIORITIZATION MATRIX

This tool (Figure 3.3; TDA, 2007) is a good visual means of gathering feedback from team members on their perceptions of different aspects of the learning community and its processes.

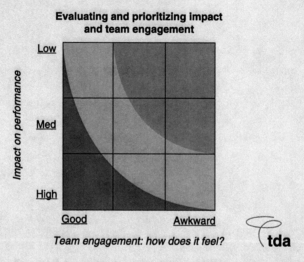

Figure 3.3 Example of prioritization matrix

Gather participants around a flipchart on which you have drawn the basic grid outline, with each axis labelled. Give the participants a list of different aspects you wish to evaluate (e.g. action learning set, fishbowl discussions, coaching, learning walks), ask them to write comments on Post-Its – using a separate one for each comment – then place each Post-It in the appropriate place on the grid.

When the flipchart is full, use coloured marker pens to draw on the coloured areas that indicate priorities for action:

- bottom left corner – ignore
- central zones – find ways to improve the process
- top right corner – continue and strengthen.

Some interesting discussion could be generated around how to tackle the central zone issues!

RESOURCE 11: ASSESSING TEAM LEARNING

This 'spot' questionnaire measures perceptions of departmental or project team members, and is double-edged: each question requires two responses so that it may be analysed in terms of the gap between frequency of use and perceived effectiveness of learning.

Tick the two boxes in each line that reflect best what you think.

Table 3.5 Frequency and effectiveness of team activities

Insert project activities you want to assess on each line below	*Very often*	*Quite often*	*Only sometimes*	*Rarely or never*	*Learn a lot*	*Learn quite a lot*	*Learn a little*	*Learn nothing*
e.g. Team meetings								

RESOURCE 12: FORCE FIELD ANALYSIS

Force-field analysis is used to map the sometimes opposing forces within an environment where change is taking place. It can be particularly useful when issues have already been identified and teams want to analyse and understand the prevailing forces, which should be dealt with and start to inform an action plan.

The tool begins with a clear statement of something regarded by a team as a problem or issue. The team also needs to make a statement of the goal or outcome that it is seeking.

The team will list those forces that drive towards the desired outcome and also the restraining forces that impede its achievement. Each of these forces is then given a score of 1 to 4 (where 1 is a weak force and 4 a strong one). Calculating the cumulative totals of each of the driving and restraining forces can give the team an indication of which set of forces would prevail in the current environment.

Once this analysis of things 'as they are at the moment' has been carried out, a team can begin to look at what actions can be taken to build on restraining forces and reduce restraining ones.

What are the main driving and restraining forces? List them here, and score each one (NCSL, 2006).

Driving forces promoting change	*Restraining forces resisting change*
1	
2	
3	
4	

RESOURCE 13: FOCUS GROUPS

A focus group is a method for consulting with end users in order to gain insights into people's attitudes, understandings and perceptions that may not be possible on a one-to-one basis. Being in a group situation can help to gain a variety of views and perceptions that are stimulated through interaction, group discussion and reflection. Views can be explored in greater depth and more quickly than with some other consultation methods.

A point to bear in mind is that there will be a significant time factor involved in finding participants and maintaining their involvement. This should be factored into your project.

How to run a focus group

Invite a relatively small but representative group of between 10 and 20 people. This could be a mixed group of students and relevant staff. A focus group session typically lasts from about one to two hours and is run by a facilitator. This should be someone with good interpersonal skills who can maintain the group's focus.

Hold the focus group in a comfortable room with seating that enables everyone to see each other. Plan to record the session or have a co-facilitator who can take notes. It is important to be clear about the objective of the focus group from the start, and it is helpful to have a minimum of around five or six questions. The questions should be clear and related to the subject and content of the focus group theme, which participants need to be informed about beforehand. The objective and questions, along with an agenda, can be sent out in advance so that participants can prepare themselves for the focus group.

It is important to consider the membership of the focus group and select people who are likely to take part actively. It is the responsibility of the facilitator to ensure that everyone gets an opportunity to participate. You will also need to consider the specific needs of group members.

A few other points for facilitators to consider are as follows.

- Give people time and space to speak.
- Be aware of any specific needs among the participants.
- Don't make the focus group too structured – look for spontaneity.
- Ensure discussion stays on track.
- Pose specific questions to encourage everyone to participate.
- Don't get directly involved in the discussion.
- Make sure no single individual dominates the group.
- Agree a set of ground rules before starting.

RESOURCE 14: FISHBOWL DISCUSSION

The fishbowl is used to encourage discussion among group members to explore issues and share opinions. It requires two circles to be made – one inner circle and one outer. This can be arranged with chairs to sit on or simply with spaces on the floor. One chair or space is intentionally left vacant in the inner circle. Participants then sit in either the inner or the outer circle.

Only the members of the inner circle may speak during the fishbowl activity. If someone in the outer circle wants to speak, he or she goes to the one vacant chair or space. He or she vacates the chair when they are tapped on the shoulder by another person from the outer circle who wants to take their place.

Ground rules should be established by the facilitator to match the purpose of the activity. Examples of ground rules are as follows.

- A participant must state an idea and support it with a fact or opinion; agree with a speaker and add supporting information; or disagree with a speaker and offer a fact or opinion to refute his/her argument.
- No one may interrupt a speaker.
- No speaker may speak a second time on a topic until all persons wishing to speak on the topic have had a chance.

How to use a fishbowl

The outer circle may be assigned to listen, take notes, and observe. If a person from the outer circle wishes to speak or ask a question, he or she must come forward and exchange chairs with a member of the inner circle.

As people swap positions and get their chance to speak, so the views of all people are gradually recorded, as are the interactions between people. The role of the facilitator can involve:

- presenting the topic for discussion
- asking open-ended questions
- encouraging, harmonizing, clarifying, and, in some cases, limiting statements
- establishing time parameters and notifying the group as the deadline approaches
- helping participants to process the activity by asking the following questions:
  o What surprised you about the discussion?
  o Have you changed your mind about anything in response to the discussion?

RESOURCE 15: BACKCASTING

This tool can be used most effectively when moving a team from an agreed shared vision towards implementation. It involves developing a detailed view of the future that your leadership will need to bring about if the vision is to be realized.

Stage 1 (10 minutes)

Allow the group to re-engage with the shared vision by thinking about the preferred future that has been agreed.

Stage 2 (20–30 minutes)

Ask small groups to describe the key differences between:

- the policy/project or subject area now and in the preferred future
- the wider external environment now and in the preferred future
- the internal environment now and in the future.

Stage 3 (45 minutes)

Identify the key stages to achieving the future.

- Build a timeline between now and the preferred future.
- Describe the key events and steps that need to occur to achieve the preferred future.
- Map them onto a timeline displayed on flipchart sheets.

Stage 4 (45 minutes)

Split into breakout groups.

- Brainstorm trends, drivers and events that might have an impact on the key steps towards delivering the future.
- Capture trends, drivers and events on Post-Its.
- Map Post-Its on a 2 × 2 matrix according to whether they are barriers (to achieving the preferred vision) or enablers (towards achieving the preferred vision); and whether they are in your control or out of your control.

Stage 5 (40 minutes)

Four breakout groups, as follows.

- Group 1 focuses on barriers in our control:

  o What are they?
  o How will they affect our ability to deliver the preferred future?
  o What steps do we need to take to remove them?

- Group 2 focuses on enablers in our control:

  o What are they?
  o How will they affect our ability to deliver the preferred future?
  o How do we harness them to strengthen the strategy?

- Group 3 focuses on barriers outside our control:

  o What are they?
  o How will they affect our ability to deliver the preferred future?
  o What can we do to minimize their impact?

- Group 4 focuses on enablers outside our control:

  o What are they?
  o How will they affect our ability to deliver the preferred future?
  o How can we harness them to strengthen the strategy?

Stage 6 (20 minutes)

Feedback and discussion.

Stage 7 (15 minutes)

Next steps:

- What are they?
- To be done when?
- By whom?

RESOURCE 16: VIDEO OR PHOTO EVALUATION

This activity may take a number of forms; it is particularly revealing when students work in groups with a camera to record places or people that, in terms of their learning experience, are most engaging or motivating and those that are least so.

It allows a project team to see itself through a different lens. It is an enjoyable activity for students, and can be empowering. It can clearly be used to document a very wide range of perceptions of staff, too.

The activity is limited by the medium to what can be seen and by the perceptiveness of those with the camera. In some cases, it may be threatening and reveal things some people would rather not have exposed.

CASE STUDY 5: UNIVERSITY OF ARIZONA
Creating a community of leaders

University of Arizona facts

The University of Arizona was established in 1885. It is a public university which provides a comprehensive, high-quality education that engages students in discovery through research and broad-based scholarship. The aim of the university is to empower graduates to be leaders in solving complex societal problems. In 2011/12 it had 12,053 employees, offered 160 degree programmes and had a headcount of 39,236 students. The University of Arizona is one of the world's top 100 universities and is ranked among the 20 leading public universities within America. It remains accessible to and engages with its students and its community.

Background

The University of Arizona values its commitment to high-quality research, teaching and learning, and its close connections with the local community. While it continues to value the expertise that externals bring to the organization and does recruit internationally through a consultation process, in 2009 it was recognized that leaders who were being employed from outside the university were struggling to come to terms with the unique culture and differentiation that the University of Arizona was trying to achieve (see below). The university therefore recognized that more needed to be done to induct these individuals into the organization, but also that it should seek to ensure that all employees understood the underpinning philosophy, values and vision of the organization, and that support mechanisms should be put in place to develop the leaders at all levels within the organization.

Coming to terms with culture and differentiation

Organ rejection, the process by which a foreign body is rejected by its host, is an apt metaphor for thinking about the experience many organizations face when bringing in new leaders after an external search. While organ and tissue transplants are designed to improve health, or even save lives, they can actually cause irritation or even life threatening infection. At the University of Arizona, we observed several instances in which new leaders failed to appreciate or acclimate to our culture, thereby weakening our organizational immune system. Over time we began to question whether our bias for external leaders was truly benefiting the university's long-term health. (Vaillancourt, 2012)

Leadership programmes within the University of Arizona

A comprehensive provision of leadership development programmes has been developed at the university. These include the following.

- **Managing the UA Way** which is a one-day orientation targeted at managers and supervisors who are new to their roles or new to the university. Topics include workforce planning, performance management, and fostering a positive work environment.
- **New Heads of Seminar Series** which is targeted at new academic department heads and is the longest running programme. This four-session programme begins by exploring the dynamics of moving into an administrative role and is followed by sessions that address budgeting, faculty mentoring, promotion and tenure, and building a positive organizational culture.
- **Managing in Action** programme which is targeting middle managers. The programme concentrates on creating a high-performance culture. Effective organizational communication and ethics, morality and values are included in the eight-seminar programme.
- **Leadership and Innovation Reading Group** which is targeted at deans and vice-presidents and is known within the organization as the Book Club. It was launched in an effort to bring university leaders together around new leadership ideas. The Book Club promotes the books selected by this group in order to encourage others in the community to consider the ideas under discussion. Books discussed in 2012 included *The Innovative University* by Clayton Christensen and Henry Eyring, *The Advantage: Why Organizational Health Trumps Everything Else in Business* by Patrick Lencioni, and *Start With Why: How Great Leaders Inspire Everyone to Take Action* by Simon Sinek.
- **The Academic Leadership Institute** which targets current and potential senior leaders.

The Academic Leadership Institute programme is now in its third year and has seen the most significant change within the organization. Participation in this programme is not only for academic members of staff; 'academic' in the title is to denote that any leader is leading an academic institution. This is a year-long programme and targets academic departmental heads, associate deans, departmental directors and shared governance leaders. It is designed to build leadership capacity, deepen knowledge about the university's priorities and support the creation of professional support networks. It consists of a two-day orientation with a considerable amount of analysis of the individual's personal attributes and traits, including a 360-degree assessment tool and a Myers-Briggs Type Indicator diagnostic so that the individual can come to terms with their own personal leadership style. The programme is delivered on four individual days throughout the year, and aims to build skills in topics such as achieving agreements, cultivating allies, expanding influence, leading change in innovation and overcoming conflict. These individual days are complemented by breakfast programmes with business, community and government leaders to address topics ranging from state and federal government relations to forging corporate partnerships, to institutional strategy and organizational branding. Participants also receive executive coaching and peer coaching.

Of the 75 delegates who have been on the programme to date, more than a third have gained promotion or been offered leadership opportunities (e.g., committee chairs) within the organization. The programme is open to employees within the organization; applicants require endorsement from their line manager and a letter of support. To date there have been three times more applicants for the programme each year than can be accommodated.

Key successes of the programme have been:

- the building of confidence among the organizational leaders;
- obtaining baseline skills for high-level leadership positions;
- understanding the context of the organization within the community, both nationally and internationally;
- reinforced commitment and loyalty to the organization and its development, networking within the organization;
- understanding the key components of the organization and how it works;
- the formation of strong networks that enable leaders to call on colleagues to help resolve issues. The networking aspect of the provision has been seen as the greatest single benefit within the organization.

The Human Resources Department has indicated the benefits to the institution as being a significant retention tool for key staff within the organization, a re-energizing of staff, a reduction in the amount of expenditure involved in appointing external staff to the institution, and a reduction in the amount spent in orienting leaders to its culture. As a follow-up from the programme, leaders are also offered the opportunity to continue with their executive coaching.

Of the people who have participated in the programme, four have left the organization; as an example, one of these is now the director of the county health department and is an important ambassador for the university.

Conclusion

The University of Arizona believes in providing its employees with the leadership skills to help the individual and the organization achieve their goals. It is conscious (as Rubin, 2007 stated – see below) that employees in academic institutions may not have the management and leadership skills required and that all employees need to understand fully the strategic direction of the organization and its culture. The university fulfils its commitment to establishing leaders from within the organization and to ensuring that all employees are given an opportunity to gain the leadership development skills that the organization needs for the future.

> For reasons that are difficult to understand, leadership development has historically not been the priority in higher education that it has been in other sectors . . . The assumption seems to be that leadership and managerial capabilities will emerge and develop naturally among those who have excelled in academic or technical areas.
>
> (Rubin, 2007: 138)

Leadership and managerial capabilities in higher education: Questions

1   Would such a radical refocusing be beneficial to your organization?
2   What key ideas would you take from this case study that would make a positive difference in your organization?

Case study developed by Allison M. Vaillancourt, Vice President for Human Resources and for Institutional Effectiveness, University of Arizona, and Professor Dawn Forman.

4 Emotionally intelligent organizational cultures

Applying emotional intelligence to designing opportunities for engagement

Much of the early work on identifying emotional intelligence and analysing its application to organizational dynamics is attributed to Goleman (1995). Subsequent refinements and collaborative work with others (Goleman et al., 2002) linked emotional intelligence to approaches to leadership, and enabled definition of a set of leadership competencies. These are divided into personal competence (how people manage themselves individually) and social competence (how people manage relationships).

The starting point for many leadership development programmes covers the first of four domains of emotional intelligence identified by Goleman et al. (2002): the personal competence domain of self-awareness. Diagnostic instruments such as the Myers Briggs Type Indicator, FIRO-B and 360-degree feedback surveys are used to build up a picture for individual participants of how they see themselves relative to the ways they are perceived by others.

The other three emotional intelligence domains are usually addressed as part of a rounded picture used to build self-awareness. These domains also feature strongly in the content of leadership development programmes, in that it is common to find masterclasses and developmental workshops covering discrete competencies within these domains (e.g. sessions on Influencing, Building Teams, Managing Conflict or Developing Others).

However, unless the programmes are designed in such a way as to be both highly experiential and strongly feedback-intensive, the competencies are rarely actually developed during the programmes themselves. They are often described, and models are presented in order to develop conceptual understanding of what they are and why they are important, but programmes can all too easily fall short of enabling participants to practise them in an authentic setting. The challenge of practising is often left to opportunities to 'transfer' learning back in the workplace. One might question how likely it is that such opportunities actually transpire.

The other three domains are self-management (personal competence), social awareness (social competence) and relationship management (social competence).

Where individual leaders in higher education report having difficulties in the workplace, these are often described in terms of the competencies identified under relationship management, using such language as:

There are certain research professors I find it impossible to manage.

It's tough trying to get people in the department to work as a team.

How do I get a mandate to make change happen when everyone knows it's needed, yet still there's resistance?

I think it's very difficult to deal with conflict when there are so many strong egos around.

For those wishing to provide solutions to enable leaders to tackle such challenges, it is perfectly feasible to design tasks, activities and experiences that allow people to gain insights and take away valid ideas that they can implement in the workplace in order to bring about improvements in the quality of the relationships they manage. However, unless work is also done on the other two domains (self-management and social awareness), the impact in terms of relationships may well be limited.

If we look at the competencies identified by Goleman et al. for self-management, it becomes apparent that it is more difficult to 'teach' these through models and techniques. They include optimism, initiative, transparency, adaptability and emotional self-control (Goleman et al., 2002: 47–48).

The competencies of social awareness are equally impossible to impart. They depend on a combination of personality traits, value sets and a certain depth of experience to develop fully, and cannot be offered as a magic bullet to disciples of leadership, however willing they may be. The competencies are empathy, organizational awareness and a sense of service in terms of identifying and meeting the needs of others (2002: 47–48).

Nevertheless, within a strong organizational culture, it is possible to build frameworks within which people can support and challenge one another constructively. By giving attention to the design of physical spaces for dialogue, by planning specific events that bring about engagement, and through creating open processes of decision-making in which power is not wielded clandestinely, leaders can develop a climate in which emotional intelligence is both acknowledged and nurtured. This chapter demonstrates how leaders might make this happen.

Given the diversity of internal groupings in universities, and the complexities of organizational structures, it would be difficult to conceive of an entire institution demonstrating consistent levels of emotional intelligence. Stereotypical views lend themselves to ready identification of those professional services areas and academic disciplines that lend themselves comfortably to favouring emotional intelligence – and conversely to those that do not. One might argue that the university is uniquely placed to redefine such social constructs, though, and in doing so would serve the interests of its students, staff and of society as a whole. Challenging all areas of the institution to become more emotionally intelligent is perhaps one of the most powerful ways in which universities can repurpose themselves around a transformative agenda.

The importance placed on the ability of effective leaders to build relationships that lead to positive outcomes for individuals and organizations has grown in the past decade. Stein and Book (2006: 31) state that 'unsuccessful CEOs put strategy before people'. In the education sector, studies of school headteachers (NCSL, 2006) have found emotional intelligence (EI) to be highly important in determining the perceived success of individual leaders. The qualities of EI that were regarded as most important were the ability to:

- rise above personal differences
- bounce back from difficult situations/experiences
- deal with other people's anger effectively
- spot unrest/anxiety/anger swiftly and respond appropriately.

These abilities seem to be prerequisites of creating the conditions for organizational learning. Such conditions emphasize (Robinson, 2008) the importance of taking risks, demonstrating belief in others, widespread ownership of initiative, and encouragement of creativity and experimentation. In Robinson's view, followers will only trust the authenticity of leaders' behaviour when they see it personified in lived-out values. As a master storyteller, Robinson understands and harnesses the power of stories as repositories of values. In this, he is not alone.

A study of 20 senior leaders from a range of sectors in the UK (Hockey and Ley, 2010: 3) found that most of those surveyed use

> narrative and stories to share successes and motivate people and they listen to the stories within their organisations to get an understanding of how to communicate with the different employee groups and wider stakeholders. The corporate and organisational narratives they use are related to their engaging transformational leadership style.

Some of the benefits claimed (Hockey and Ley, 2010: 63) for the successful use of narrative in organizations include 'helping people buy into change, feeling energised and motivated'.

In programmes run by the Leadership Foundation, leaders taking part reported initial discomfort on being asked to identify and practise using stories in their own work, feeling that they would be denounced by colleagues in their workplaces for using a technique that might be seen as inauthentic. This seems to be indicative of the natural inclination of universities towards prioritizing cognitive intelligence and thus downplaying the significance of the affective domain.

The idea of the compassionate university is surprisingly undeveloped in the literature, despite the deeply humanistic concerns of the core work of some institutions such as widening participation, fulfilling individual potential, and contributing to the wellbeing of local communities.

CASE STUDY 6: CURTIN UNIVERSITY, WESTERN AUSTRALIA
Developing emotionally intelligent institutions by understanding the history and background of the individual

Background

Each of us lives in diverse communities that are multicultural, multi-lingual, and incorporate a range of religious and faith backgrounds. The people we live and work with have a variety of social, political and ethnic beliefs, some of which are derived from their own history or the history of their families. This rich diversity, if recognized and harmonized, can bring real strengths to any working environment. Equally, however, if the beliefs of an individual are not dealt with in a respectful way, unintended consequences can result. Equal opportunity protocols, policies and procedures, along with staff development arrangements within higher education institutions, are designed to help the appreciation of diversity and guard against prejudiced behaviour, but to be truly emotionally intelligent and to fully appreciate individual difference requires a much fuller review of the factors forming that difference.

Australia, through its reconciliation policies and development of cultural awareness, has tried to ensure that respect is given to Aboriginal people. Curtin University has embraced this development, and what started as a focus on the needs of aboriginal people has moved to an appreciation of the diversity of the many immigrant populations working and studying at the institution. In so doing Curtin has seen not only an appreciation of the difference individuals bring to an organization but also an improvement in the emotional intelligence of students and staff. Would such an approach or focus help in other countries and other contexts?

The original Indigenous population of Australia migrated from India via the 'Southern Route' around 50,000 years ago; some researchers indicate that they can trace the ancestors of the indigenous people to 125,000 years ago. The term 'Indigenous' is referring to both Aboriginal and Torres Strait Islands people as the Indigenous peoples (Torres Strait Islands people come from the islands of the Torres Strait, between the tip of Cape York in Queensland and Papua New Guinea.) The peoples of the Torres Strait have their own distinctive identity, history and cultural traditions, and many Torres Strait Islanders now live on mainland Australia.

Following white settlement Indigenous Australians were subject to a raft of legislation that restricted their movement. Nearly all aspects of their lives were regulated by government-appointed 'protectors'. In some Australian states the parents' rights were denied and the 'Chief Protector' was designated as the legal guardian of Aboriginal children.

Further legislation and government policy saw the forced removal of Aboriginal and Torres Strait Islander children from their parents. As many as one in 10 Indigenous children were forcibly removed from their families and communities in the first half of the twentieth century. The *Bringing Them Home* Report of the National Inquiry into the Separation of Aboriginal and Torres Strait Islander Children from Their Families detailed these practices and the impact they have had at both the individual and the community level (www.humanrights.gov.au/publications/bringing-them-home-stolen-children-report-1997). This removal of children has been termed the 'Stolen Generations'.

Indigenous Australians continue to be the most disadvantaged group in Australia. They have a life expectancy around 12 years less than that of other Australians (www.abs.gov.au/AUSSTATS/abs@.nsf/Lookup/4102. 0Main+Features10Mar+2011), and are only half as likely to have completed high school. They have higher rates of unemployment and there are high levels of alcohol and substance abuse (http://aboriginal.childhealthresearch. org.au). It was in the context of increasing awareness of the history of white settlement in Australia, and the impact of major inquiries including the Royal Commission into Aboriginal Deaths in Custody and the *Bringing them Home* report, that the Prime Minister offered the Apology to Aboriginal and Torres Strait Islander people (www.daa.wa.gov.au/en/ Information/The-Apology).

> I move that . . .
> We today take this first step by acknowledging the past and laying claim to a future that embraces all Australians.
> A future where this Parliament resolves that the injustices of the past must never, never happen again.
> A future where we harness the determination of all Australians, Indigenous and non-Indigenous, to close the gap that lies between us in life expectancy, educational achievement and economic opportunity.
> A future where we embrace the possibility of new solutions to enduring problems where old approaches have failed.
> A future based on mutual respect, mutual resolve and mutual responsibility.
> A future where all Australians, whatever their origins, are truly equal partners, with equal opportunities and with an equal stake in shaping the next chapter in the history of this great country, Australia.
> (The Prime Minister, the Hon. Kevin Rudd, 13 February 2008)

In 2008, Curtin University was the first university to develop and implement a Reconciliation Action Plan (RAP), committed to closing the gap in health and education outcomes between Indigenous and non-Indigenous Australians. The plan includes a commitment to indigenizing its curricula and to facilitating mutual respect and equal opportunities for all Australians (Indigenous and migrant) with equal opportunities for the future. Its Centre for Aboriginal Studies offers a series of Aboriginal cultural awareness modules that have now been embedded in the Faculty of Health Sciences curricula. These include an intercultural leadership development programme that aims to address Indigenous culture and education, assessment and moderation practices, Indigenous curriculum development, strategies for building local Indigenous community engagement and the recruitment of Indigenous teaching staff, skill building and reliance for cross-cultural teaching, and the scholarship of cross-cultural teaching and learning.

As students are introduced to Indigenous Australian history, they move through various stages of cross-cultural awareness and development as they recognize their cultural-specific world view biases, ethnicity and associated privileges (Helms, 1990). This teaching has a significant level of emotional labour, and this is particularly so for Indigenous teachers whose own identity and values are often under attack with remarks that can be racist (whether intentionally or not).

As students move along their cross-cultural continuum (Behrendt, 1996), Indigenous academics often feel most comfortable teaching within Aboriginal studies centres. In order to develop an increased number of Indigenous academics willing to teach across faculties there needs to be a scaffolding approach so that it is culturally safe for them to do so.

'Cultural safety' is a term coined by a Maori nurse, Irihapeti Ramsden, which acknowledges the crucial role of cultural awareness and reflective consideration of cultural differences in health professionals' ability to provide effective care. 'Unsafe cultural practice is any action which diminishes or disempowers cultural identity and well-being in an individual.' Ramsden, quoted in Goold (2006: 60), makes a distinction between cultural awareness, cultural safety and cultural security.

In Ramsden's definitions, awareness and safety are the foundations for attaining cultural security that directly links understandings and actions. She argues that cultural safety cannot be achieved without brokerage and protocols where: (a) all parties involved are equally important and informed (acknowledging and valuing Indigenous knowledge as equal to Western); and (b) Aboriginal context is formally recognized through the involvement of Aboriginal community and elders in providing appropriate and culturally secure practices (Coffin, 2007: 22–23).

Cultural awareness, safety and security do not just apply to the Aboriginal community and, while this may have been an obvious starting point for Curtin University, the institution has applied a number of these concepts to embrace other migrant populations, and indeed the diversity of all the people who study or are employed at the university, thus facilitating a more equitable and transparent environment for staff and students. This has been a very different approach from that of normal equal opportunities policy development that operates in many universities, but the institution has seen benefits including:

- staff and student satisfaction surveys
- increase in applications from diverse groups of staff and students
- enhanced institutional reputation.

While this is not fully tested, the institution is also seeing indications from leadership and management surveys that the emotional intelligence of staff has increased.

Questions

1 What responsibility do universities have in ensuring that staff understand cultural awareness and cultural safety?
2 Do staff understand their own privilege and how it impacts on others and their work?
3 Is it seen as important in your institution for staff and students to understand the cultural and religious heritage of your country's population?
4 Would such an understanding reshape the way in which equal opportunities are embraced within your institution?
5 Are policies and procedures the best or only way to actually achieve cultural awareness and cultural safety within an organization?
6 How is your institution embracing diversity of cultures, gender, religion, belief, and social backgrounds?

Case study developed by Professor Dawn Forman and Associate Professor Linley Lord, Curtin University, October 2012.

Reconceptualizing meetings
Creating new approaches for collective dialogue

Once, I ran a workshop in which I started by asking participants to close their eyes and picture the worst meeting they had ever witnessed in a university. I was the only one who had the opportunity to see the effect this had on those in the room, but it struck me powerfully that the reaction on everyone's face was an emotive one. A huge range was represented, including smiles, frowns, raised eyebrows and mopped foreheads.

I had anticipated drawing out from the group the factors that contributed to the awfulness of their respective meetings, and that these would lead to an analysis of dysfunction. It suddenly occurred to me how unlikely it was that those responsible for planning and chairing these meetings had actually considered the emotional outcomes that would result. I made a note to myself to plan for my own meetings as experiences rather than transactional encounters.

Most of us have learned how to conduct ourselves in meetings through long (and sometimes bitter), cumulative experience. We contribute in ways that emulate – or oppose – the behaviours of those around us. We make conscious and unconscious decisions about how to handle the deeds and utterances of others. At our worst, we might come away battle-scarred, bemused or humiliated. We may find ourselves uttering phrases such as 'I didn't have a clue what was going on there!'

At our best, however, we might take pride in the way we were able to lift the moral tone, shape a decision or influence constructive relationships. On these occasions, we're likely to say with pleasant surprise, 'Well, that went well!'

The salutary reality is that such polar opposite perceptions may well constantly be in the hearts and minds of many people who take part in our own meetings. What stops us investigating this, and what gets in the way of our doing anything about it? Often, the only barrier is one of inertia, and the only reason for ongoing complicity in maintaining the status quo is one of 'this is the way we've always done things around here'. However, fear can also be a significant factor, especially in meetings where an established sense of deference is all too clear, and where those with diminished egos and lowly standing may fear to tread.

Ryde (2013) outlines the prevailing features of deferential cultures as:

- hesitant, guarded dialogue
- division and a 'them and us' mindset
- under-utilized talent
- a fear of failure
- a passing on of responsibility
- an illusion of support for change
- ethical inconsistency
- a controlling mindset.

If these characteristics are familiar to you, but you have the potential to make changes in meetings you chair, it may be helpful to begin by building a mandate for doing things differently.

This might start by seeking anonymized feedback at the end of a meeting, for instance using Post-It notes to elicit views on how the meeting might be run differently next time, or asking participants to cite the most effective outcomes of the meeting (such as decisions taken, understanding realized, or priorities defined).

Your ability to respond to such feedback by implementing small incremental changes (and seeking further ongoing feedback on these as the changes take place) will determine the extent to which others take you seriously and are prepared to support further attempts to make your meetings more engaging, effective and democratic.

Before embarking on changes to the meetings you are involved in, it would be worth considering the experiences offered by Pearl, who advocates that all meetings need to be led, and that this does not necessarily equate to chairing or hosting them: 'If no-one else is leading, the leader is *you*' (2012: 290; emphasis in original). Pearl argues passionately against complicity in the dullness or ineffectiveness of meetings, and suggests that a starting point for change in approaches is an understanding of the typology of meetings. He lists seven categories of purposes of meetings (2012: 168):

- meeting to inform
- meeting to discuss
- meeting to decide
- meeting to (re)solve
- meeting to innovate
- meeting to sell
- meeting to meet – reinforcing social connections.

As well as pointing out the importance of clarifying the purpose(s) of a meeting when setting out the agenda, Pearl emphasizes the opportunity that exists for a leader to set the tone by stating *why* a meeting is important. This focus on the intent of the meeting (rather than a statement of its objectives) enables a clear position to be established for how the meeting can 'generate extraordinary value for everyone involved' (Pearl, 2012: 76) and create stronger commitment and motivation. These are clearly leadership challenges that call for alignment between what leaders espouse and what they actually do in practice.

Further interest can be added to meetings by the presence of special guests able to bring surprise, 'depth and richness' (Pearl, 2012: 90). One example Pearl cites is that of a client or beneficiary of an organization's services who can speak of transformative experiences brought about by the organization – numerous examples for universities come to mind, ranging from students from underprivileged backgrounds to representatives of partner bodies with which an institution has engaged.

Pearl goes on to emphasize skills that can be developed among adherents of effective meetings, including those of listening, questioning, engaging participants emotionally, debating, and reviewing the outcomes from previous meetings.

Given the opportunities that the meetings format provides for using questions effectively, it is worth considering earlier work by Ryde (2007) in which he argues convincingly that the tone and direction provided by early questions in a dialogue lead participants' thinking along narrow channels from which it is subsequently difficult to diverge. He also makes a case for a leader developing the awareness and capabilities required to challenge predominant thinking by using powerful questions to shape the conversation and channel it in new directions.

Table 4.1 Thinking channels (adapted from Ryde, 2007)

Dominant channel	Trigger questions	Likely responses
• Deficit thinking	What do you think of this?	• Finding faults and limitations
• Rational thinking	What's your analysis of this?	• Intellectually balanced views
• Binary thinking	What's our view on this?	• Either/or thinking; one correct solution
• Common sense	What are the options here?	• Obvious/everybody knows we should . . .
• Equity thinking	Are we being consistent here?	• Fairness by empathizing with potentially disadvantaged parties

Ryde states that there are five dominant thinking channels deployed in everyday life in organizations, and that each of these channels can be identified by the kinds of questions used to initiate and reinforce them (Table 4.1).

Readers will be able to identify which of these channels are most prevalent in their own institutions, but it is clear that some of them appeal directly to the values and behaviours around which scholarly traditions are based, including those associated with critical thinking, reasoned argument and emancipation. However, while Ryde supports the efficacy of these dominant ways of thinking, he also identifies what he calls 'shadow channels' (Table 4.2), to which a skilled leader has recourse when wishing to generate a wider variety of constructive thinking in a conversation or meeting. Each of the dominant channels has its respective opposite or shadow – and each is likely to generate a very different set of responses from participants.

You may wish to encourage colleagues to develop their awareness of, and ability to spot, the various dominant thinking channels at work in meetings they attend.

Table 4.2 Dominant and shadow channels (adapted from Ryde, 2007)

Dominant channel	Shadow channel	Trigger questions
• Deficit thinking	• Strength-based thinking	What's working well?/ What are we proud of in this department?
• Rational thinking	• Feeling thinking	What emotional effect does this idea have on us?
• Binary thinking	• Reintegrated thinking	What if we could have both a better and a cheaper student experience?
• Common sense	• Insight thinking	What do we know from our research evidence that matters here?
• Equity thinking	• 360-degree thinking	How would (all) others in the university see this?

Following a discussion on what you learn through observation and reflection, you could then give a card similar to those below to particular individuals, and ask them to try incorporating the specific shadow channel into their own repertoire of meeting behaviours, as appropriate (adapted from Ryde, 2007).

Strength-based thinking involves a search for what works well in order to understand why, and in order to strengthen it further. It builds confidence and injects energy into conversations. It involves taking an appreciative perspective to what we experience.

- What has been working most successfully?
- What particular features have been most helpful?
- Where have we made most progress?

Feeling thinking acknowledges that emotions are important in workplace decision-making, and encourages and provides permission to contribute emotional data to a discussion.

- What does our instinct tell us?
- How do we feel about this problem?
- What is our emotional response to this?
- What is the likely impact of this on others?

Reintegrated thinking tries to avoid either/or approaches to finding solutions. It involves asking how it might be useful to think about ways to integrate seemingly incongruous possibilities. As a result, it can lead to creative outcomes.

- How could we have both of these possibilities?
- What strengths do these opposing positions share?
- What would it actually be like if we could have both?

Insight thinking draws on existing practical experience or proven expertise in order to elicit solutions to problems. This requires an honest exploration of what people really know, and demands that evidence be sought in support of finding real insights.

- How has this problem been solved in similar or different contexts?
- What do we know, from experience, matters here?
- What expertise can we apply to this challenge?

360-degree thinking involves seeing a situation simultaneously from many perspectives, and trying to understand changes of perception that result. This strengthens decision-making considerably, by providing insights and confidence to make progress.

- How would other parties or stakeholders see this?
- Who might see it differently, and how would they justify their viewpoint?
- Could we hear all of the potential perspectives on this?

RESOURCE 17: GO-AROUND DISCUSSIONS IN MEETINGS

Another approach to handling meetings differently lies in using turn-taking in order to democratize a meeting by giving equal voice to all those taking part. This can be productive in that it reduces the airtime given to the 'usual suspects' who would otherwise dominate a meeting. It also counters those who reserve their comments until the end of a discussion when, having heard everyone's views, they might sabotage the outcome with a tactical verbal torpedo or two.

Turn-taking is arguably at its purest in the practices advocated by Kline's (1999) 'Thinking Environment'. Here, taking a strict rotational order, participants in a meeting give a single short answer in response to a stimulus question. Ground rules are clearly established before beginning, including the expectation that when one person is speaking, others look at them with interest and do not pass judgement or comment in any way on what they hear. A typical opening question might be:

What could we be doing to help this organization through turbulent times?

Having heard all the responses round the table, the participants can then be divided into pairs, and asked to spend five minutes each way exploring the prompt question further. Here, there are clearly two distinct roles in a five-minute slot – those of questioner and of respondent. The responsibility of the questioner is to continue to show rapt interest in what the respondent says, without offering any commentary or further discussion. During the five minutes, which can seem remarkably intense for both parties, the questioner simply uses each time the respondent finishes stating an idea as an opportunity to repeat the same question:

> What *else* could we be doing to help this organization through turbulent times?

The respondent, meanwhile, generates 10 or more good ideas spontaneously. When both slots are complete, all participants are invited back into the original configuration around the table, and asked to reflect for a minute or two on the best idea they had during their five minutes. They then feed this back into a turn-taking round, offering the idea they liked best. Although there will be individuals who insist that their first idea was their best, the point is usually well taken that most meetings comprise utterances that are likely to be the first thought, and not necessarily the thought of the highest possible quality, to enter the minds of the contributors.

At this point, a group can decide whether or not to use the responses as the basis for committing to individual actions, or to determine collective intentions for the team or working group.

It is worth considering how to overcome the risk of groups being 'over-cohesive' – once people get skilled at working together collaboratively, groupthink can set in, meaning that a team fails to be sufficiently challenging or creative during meetings. It may be helpful to introduce a process whereby those who chair meetings can improve the quality of critical thinking in the discourse.

RESOURCE 18: USING OBSERVATIONS OF MEETINGS

Ainscow et al. (1994) suggest setting up a system for observing meetings that are typical of departmental life, then reflecting on and discussing the observations before deciding appropriate courses of action.

They identify six behaviours that are indicative of highly cohesive groups that do not demonstrate critical thinking:

- stereotyping of outsiders
- assuming moral superiority over outsiders
- assuming win/lose situation [in relation to encounters with outsiders]
- pressurizing a colleague to agree [with the group]
- pressing for unanimity
- withholding information that might change the course of the discussion. (1994: 109)

An observer records the number of occurrences of each of these behaviours during the course of a meeting, noting the participant responsible, and the impact the specific occurrence had on the group.

A second observer simultaneously records the occurrences of a set of behaviours associated with effective group performance:

- clarifying the group's goals, so that all members understand these; modifying and redefining goals where necessary so that these reflect the understandings and individual goals of members;
- establishing parity between group members, so that during discussions all members are able to participate fully and can assume a leadership role when appropriate;
- ensuring that authority (position-based) does not become a more important factor than information (knowledge-based) in decision making;
- drawing on a range of decision-making processes, rather than trying to 'standardize' the way the group approaches decisions. This allows for a matching of decisions approach with type of issue;
- exploring differences and being prepared to engage in conflict; the group is committed to *resolving* conflict rather than *avoiding* it;
- communication is open, and members are encouraged to express feelings and speculations as well as 'facts';
- group members reflect from time to time on the way the group is operating, evaluating its effectiveness and making changes in methods and approaches where necessary. (1994: 110)

Ainscow et al. suggest that the most effective way to make use of the data gathered from these observations is to produce a set of guidelines for those who lead or chair groups across the department. They advise on keeping the guidelines short (no more than one side of A4) and focused on behaviour. This enables a code of practice to be defined and refined at department level, and allows for values, some of which may be particular to certain academic disciplines or professional backgrounds, to be reflected in such a code. The focus on critical reflection is likely to appeal to those working in universities.

Experimenting with meetings in these ways clearly carries risks, in that it challenges facets of the prevailing culture, and may be read by others as subversive or destabilizing. It may also be seen as a means of wielding power, and thus should not be undertaken without placing it in a context of what it is that you as a leader are trying to bring about – and most importantly, what the benefits are likely to be for those involved.

Introducing small changes incrementally may prove more successful, as will involving others in providing feedback on how you introduce a new approach and how this is perceived by others. Asking an observer to notice the effect on other people allows you to focus on the task itself, rather than trying to gauge its effect at the same time.

Showing empathy and consideration
Planning for emotional and social outcomes

Prevailing models of influencing styles identify contrasts between 'push' approaches, in which the influencer attempts to be the dynamic force creating the impetus to move, and 'pull' styles, where the other party chooses to move towards the influencer's objectives. Meetings in universities are arguably more likely to draw on push styles, since these meetings are often driven by surface assumptions that they operate rationally, using the academic's trade tools of reasoned argument, critical thinking and professional judgement. Prowess in applying the requisite skills can be honed to a fine art, and when applied in the deeply political contexts of structural and ideological rivalries can lead to dangerously volatile situations. While such meetings can be a powerful training ground for resilience, they can also take their toll emotionally, and we can probably all think of those figures in our own institutions whom others take on at their own peril.

Applying some empathy to people who display apparently hostile behaviours (and who on occasion defend these as examples of 'academic freedom' in action), it may well be that they feel they have valid causes for defending themselves, or that they have had little prior opportunity to express themselves in ways that convey emotional intelligence. Indeed, it may well be that those setting up the meetings in which these behaviours arise are complicit (intentionally or otherwise) in creating atmospheres that foster toxic tendencies.

Other examples of 'push' styles in use at university meetings include instances where power is asserted in order to move towards a decision or agreement. These might involve positional power related to the hierarchical status of individuals, or their ability to provide conditional access to resources. On the other hand, it might be a more personal source of influencing power due to the reputational standing attributed to members of elites who are considered to be thought leaders.

Leaders who are seen as effective in chairing meetings are able to draw on a repertoire of influencing styles in order to facilitate successful outcomes. This includes making skilful use of 'push' styles where these are appropriate.

It also calls for capability in influencing the emotional climate of a meeting and giving attention to motivating participants and building relationships. This implies using practices that lead to collaborative patterns of behaviour on the part of participants.

RESOURCE 19: PLANNING MEETING OUTCOMES

It can be helpful to set up a meeting in ways that make clear that you expect it to be focused on achieving particular outcomes. These might relate to decisions to be taken, or priorities to be agreed. Alternatively, they may be set in a wider strategic context and include intended outcomes concerning understanding or evaluation, for instance. An example is given in Table 4.3.

Table 4.3 Example of meeting plan

Agenda item	Desired outcome
Degree ceremonies	Joy and anticipation in celebrating students' successes
Diversity and Equality Strategy for the Department	Commitment to fundamental changes in power structures and working cultures
Impact of student fee increases	Realization of importance to the whole department of building rapport and engagement with all students
Vice-Chancellor's Question Time	Potential empowerment in voicing priorities and concerns that may be acted upon

There is no suggestion here that you should publish your desired outcomes in the agenda; the key point is that you dedicate some time and energy to noting for yourself the emotional outcomes that you intend from the decisions that might be taken, or the messages that are to be communicated. Do remember to reflect on the impact of having planned for your desired outcomes.

Mastering self-regulation
How leaders build a repertoire of approaches that work in academic environments

In order to build social capital in universities and their constituent departments, it is important to consider the other forms of capital that have substantial weight in higher education, such as physical capital (based on resources), human capital (on skills and capabilities), symbolic capital (characteristics that build and affirm identity) and, of course, political capital (Bourdieu, 2008).

Effective emotional intelligence is unlikely to develop successfully unless sufficient political intelligence is also acquired. One model that often appeals to professionals in higher education is that of Baddeley and James (1987), in which people's behaviour in organizational settings is characterized by the extent to which they demonstrate interests in their own individual good or the collective good, and by how able and willing they are to read the political environment.

Those whose interest is purely individual and who are unable to understand the politics of their institution or department are characterized as inept, while highly politicized, individually focused people are depicted as clever or cunning. Those who cling together in a herd and cannot read the political environment are unsurprisingly deemed innocent or naïf.

The collectively motivated, politically mature leader would naturally wish to aspire to the category described as wise. Here, people are seen to act with integrity in the interests of a meaningful purpose, and are clearly able to navigate a turbulent environment.

In universities, having such political intelligence is likely to act as a prerequisite to being able to deploy emotional intelligence without being seen as immature or lacking in credibility. The wise leader is characterized as knowing the organization well (in terms of both overt and covert structures and processes), and able to make procedures work. They are also likely to be co-operative in orientation, good at sharing information and connecting ideas and people, doing so successfully by being aware of the viewpoints and needs of other people. Finally, the wise leader is able to reflect, to learn from failure, and to listen with skill and consideration.

Learning how to apply such political intelligence involves mastery of what Goleman et al. (2002) term self-regulation: managing one's internal states, impulses and resources. There is a clear sense of being able to take responsibility for one's own performance, and not to find fault or excuses in the shortcomings of other people or of the environment. This involves learning how to hold back on your impulses, and overcome engrained habits. Goleman et al. argue that 'practicing self-control to the point of mastery, what was once an effort becomes automatic' (2002: 204).

There are some simple approaches from the domain of Neuro-Linguistic Programming that might be practically helpful in developing greater self-regulation. These include techniques for building rapport by matching body posture, voice tonality and choice of language with those with whom one seeks to engage (Agness, 2013: 157–161).

CASE STUDY 7: DE MONTFORT UNIVERSITY
World cafés

Background

De Montfort University (DMU) believes passionately that universities are a public good through transformation of lives, through the places in which their students and staff live and work, and through sharing their discoveries for the wider benefit of society. DMU is a community in which all staff and students learn, develop and contribute through partnerships to that shared experience. Home to over 27,000 students and around 2800 staff, DMU is a vibrant and transformational institution in which to study and work.

The problem

In July 2010, the newly appointed Vice-Chancellor, Professor Dominic Shellard, set out his early thoughts on a new vision for the university and a commitment to consult with as many colleagues as possible regarding its content. This led to an unprecedented and far-reaching period of consultation within the university and externally with key partners.

Human Resources (HR) was given the responsibility for engaging staff and stakeholders on the proposed vision, to ensure that the eventual outcome considered the respective views and shared ownership.

The university's approach

Based on the World Café concept, initial engagement centred on a series of Vision Cafés, bringing together a mix of academic and professional services staff with an additional café for students. World Café is renowned for creating a collaborative and informal environment enabling idea sharing. Approximately 20% of the workforce took part in the Vision Cafés.

The objectives for the cafés were:

- to provide a genuine opportunity for employees and stakeholders to shape the future direction of the university
- to engage a diverse range of staff, students and stakeholders to elicit views and shared ownership of the final Mission and Vision
- to create an environment crossing occupational/hierarchical boundaries, to encourage colleagues to work collaboratively.

In total five Vision Cafés were held, with 50% of participants nominated by Pro Vice-Chancellors/Deans and Directors, and remaining places offered to volunteers across the institution. A training room was transformed to replicate an authentic and informal café-style environment. The project team recruited credible colleagues from across the institution to be trained to undertake café and table host roles. The training equipped the hosts to generate and document meaningful debate. In parallel, a series of internal communications was devised to engage staff and deliver a consistent message from the Vice-Chancellor – that engagement was genuine and outcomes from Vision Café were expected to be pivotal in shaping the Mission and Vision of the university.

Contributor input was instantly captured on tablecloths during Café events and evaluation of the process captured by participants writing their views on wall-boards under headings 'What's Hot' and 'What's Not' (replicating a five-point Likert scale).

Following the cafés an e-engagement process commenced for staff unable to attend a café event. Governors and key stakeholders also engaged in this way. E-engagement responses attracted as much interest as the cafés.

The outcome

The Vision Café concept generated enthusiasm and vibrancy across the university in ways not experienced before. Feedback boards unanimously reflected how these events had captured the imagination and enthusiasm of employees: 'Great to see people so passionate about DMU', 'Great to be asked opinion – boosted staff morale', 'Good to be involved – feel valued!'. The Vice-Chancellor also received unsolicited e-mails and tweets.

As a direct result of the feedback from the Vision Café process the Mission and Vision were substantially revised, demonstrating that views counted and the final product was something the entire university could 'own'.

A further tangible measure of success is the enabling effect that the cafés have had in facilitating staff across the institution to identify and understand the strategies required to gain differentiation in the marketplace. The university now has a Mission and Vision that staff understand, support and believe in. This has become vital for the success of the university's strategy moving forward.

The Mission and Vision provided the foundation for the development of a new strategic plan and a framework for decision-making.

One of the interesting elements of this project was its boldness. The World Café concept was unknown to the university, the plans of the newly appointed Vice-Chancellor were largely unknown to staff and it was difficult to gauge how successful the concept might be – all risks to a new Vice-Chancellor, Executive Board and HR Directorate.

The project was executed in a very short time span; the first Café held just four weeks after the initial project group meeting and at minimal cost. It was important to the project group that in the current climate, staff saw that these events had negligible financial implication. This was achieved through effective project management, clear leadership and collaborative working both within HR and across the institution.

Internal communication is also worthy of note. The university had not previously engaged with employees on such a wide scale and on such a pivotal matter – particularly in such an open and transparent way. E-mail communication and carefully crafted guidance documents were written to excite and engage staff and to deliver a consistent message. The final Mission and Vision are testimony to this.

Due to the success of Vision Café, 12 months later the Executive Board commissioned HR to deliver a staff engagement project to develop a set of shared values to underpin the university's approach in working together on realizing key strategic priorities. A series of Values Cafés commenced and devised this set of values.

Further information about the World Café concept can be found at www. theworldcafe.com/method.html

Questions

1   How would the World Café or Vision Café 12 concepts work in your organization?
2   How would you start to introduce such a process?
3   What would you see as the advantages of such a process in your organization?

Case study developed by Sarah Allen, Senior HR Partner and Vincent Cornelius, Training and Development Advisor, DeMontfort University, May 2013.

5 'When do we get to do feedback?'

Intrinsic feedback
How giving and seeking feedback is intrinsic to practices and behaviours throughout an organizational unit

I was fortunate enough in 2013 to flip roles, and become a participant on a leadership development programme run by another organization. In the first five minutes, our group of 20 was told in no uncertain terms to expect a week that would be 'feedback-intensive'. The journey we were embarking on would take us to uncomfortable places.

Applying sound principles of instructional design, the programme took us through a rich range of experiences, starting with a simulation. We spent a day running a well-conceived manufacturing company at a turning-point in its strategic direction. Although we needed to take some substantive business decisions, the learning was entirely about our behaviours. How we established and developed working relationships, how we attended to values and culture in the part of the company we ran, and how effective others perceived our leadership to be – this was the stuff of the feedback the programme director had talked about.

The quality of this feedback was phenomenal. It was as far removed as it's possible to be from a cursory slot of constructive criticism sandwiched between layers of appreciation.

First, we spent half an hour completing an i-Pad-based questionnaire ahead of an afternoon's discussion on our team's performance. Then we were set what was for me was the most challenging task of the week – writing feedback sheets on each of the other six people in one's team, each one of which had to be evidenced by three or four examples of behaviour or language in specific situations. What was more, in every case we had to describe the perceived impact of each example on ourselves or on others.

The next day was entirely spent processing this feedback in depth. It culminated in a 25-minute feedback round for each individual, for which we were given a digital recorder for us to take away what our peers gave us. After hearing six pieces of individual feedback, our group facilitator drew on several pages of observation notes to give us her views on the leadership impact we'd made, with some very sharply observed points (*How had she even seen when I said that? I never even knew she was there!*). This was powerful learning, and led to plentiful thinking on how we handle feedback on the Leadership Foundation's programmes.

While writing this part of the book, I felt impelled to go to my digital recorder and remind myself, with some trepidation, of the feedback day. I switched it on, and was both relieved and transported back to the sense of flow I experienced during the programme. I heard one of my colleagues telling me that the first thing I'd done was to 'spark an energy to start'. I was ready to engage with what was to come.

As I continued to listen to the recording, I remembered why I'd experienced some anxiety before returning to my feedback session. Charissa, a plant manager from Colorado, had delivered some frank perspectives:

> I felt that you were very approachable and easy to talk to. I didn't feel that you were absorbing what I had to say. I felt like you were giving me time because that's what you needed to do as a manager but you were getting all your decision-makings from [my line manager] and on up the food chain. So as far as your demeanour I thought that it was really pleasant – I just didn't feel like I was getting my point across . . . It's like you are right now, you're listening – and *maybe you are* – don't think I don't think you're listening but: I guess I kind of just felt that you were a Yes man. Your wheels were turning somewhere else . . . It was really . . . 'I'm doing this because I need to do this, this is my team, but I really need to be in my Executive meeting or getting data back from them.' And then, when you were supposed to meet with us at 1.15 and you were late – but you graciously explained to us why you were late – but I could feel you felt bad about not being at our meeting on time. But I didn't feel you did enough to make sure you were *at* the meeting on time – that you let your Executive meeting overrule what you needed to come back and do with your team . . . and when you *did* get back with us and meet with us, it was: we started talking to you but then it was wasted breath for me because you guys had already made your decisions in that meeting and we were going to wait till 2 o'clock and then we were going to get it. So it wasn't really a good time to come back and meet with us, 'cause the decisions were already made. And that's kind of a let-down.

This was close to the bone, and a reminder of my need to prioritize attention to some of my own interpersonal skills. In fact, it was a very direct set of feedback on the very issue that I had feared was an example of my own underperformance over many years as a manager. In over 20 years of managing, however, I had not asked for feedback on this – nor had anyone given me any. Listening back to this recorded feedback from the programme on several subsequent occasions has always led to a sharp intake of breath, and to discomfort. It also leads on each listening to further determination to continue addressing this aspect of my behaviour on a daily basis.

Later, I was ready to hear what other colleagues had had to say. Waves of pleasure bathed my cortex as I listened to the feedback from my boss in the simulated company. I appreciated the more intangible qualities that the 'president' had identified in me through specific examples of my behaviour:

First thing in the morning you came in, we were in the office together, you were very upbeat and just had this incredibly positive attitude and I thought . . . it lifted me and it made me feel like 'this is gonna be a good day, and we will accomplish some things' and so I think that disposition does well for you and carries you a long way. The second situation that came to mind is that maybe 20 minutes later you wanted to talk about the lawsuit. You kind of took some time quickly to make sure that that got covered, and it did. But I guess I appreciated your focus on the need and the detail of getting that accomplished . . . I felt that you were very engaged at that point into the process and into the business and again that built confidence. I felt a lot of confidence in you and what you were doing because of how you approached that and how we resolved that and your preparation for it. My third biggest moment was that somewhere late morning we were sitting in the break room – we'd just had a Sales and Marketing meeting – and we just kind of, the two of us for whatever reason we were just sitting there and, um, we had this conversation about the possibilities of some change and, erm – it wasn't specific and it wasn't necessarily detailed but your eye contact, your non-verbal communication – that process – to me, I felt that there was a connection and even though I didn't specifically start to draw out what some of those opportunities were, it was very obvious that there were things that you had seen in the course of the day. I guess I felt at that point it added to the energy of what I was seeing or experiencing in some of the other informal meetings and I just . . . it's great sometimes to be able to communicate that way and not say – just let things evolve a bit. I just thought that was a very interesting experience that was kind of unusual 'cause I don't have that very often, but a very enjoyable day and I appreciated working with you.

This was a fascinating articulation of what I too recalled as a special moment that somehow transcended the transactional or even strategic conversations that had dominated most of the simulated business day. There was a sense of flow and intuition in our conversation that felt at the time as though it represented a turning-point for the organization in which we were both senior managers. It was particularly unusual to hear my president feeding this back to me with such sensitivity, and describing the conversation in ways that indicated that he clearly valued it. In terms of managing this particular relationship, I had clearly been able to apply some influence and to build an effective bond of rapport with my boss. At the same time, his own ability to apply empathy, transparency and emotional self-control had impressed me at the time – and was demonstrated all the more powerfully in this situation of the recording by his ability to reflect and offer developmental feedback.

The emotional rollercoaster on which I was taken during that 25-minute recording was not only a reflection of the strength of the relationships we had built up during an intensive week of learning together. It was also a sign of how rare it is to give and receive extensive and specific feedback on our behaviours. This missed opportunity seems to represent a vastly underused potential organizational resource. It is part of the picture of releasing huge quantities of motivation and discretional effort from our colleagues – and it is surely the responsibility of leaders to model effective feedback practices.

King and Santana argue for the importance of intensive feedback in leadership development programmes on the grounds that it enables leaders 'to develop action plans to leverage that knowledge for greater effectiveness in their work and personal lives' (2010: 97). They refer to the importance of the environment in which the feedback is given being safe and supportive, and this clearly applies to the climate that needs to established by leaders in order to make feedback in the workplace successful, rather than a blunt instrument with damaging potential.

In universities, there is a spectrum of activities that can be used as the basis for observing colleagues in action, and thus for gathering data that could be used to provide feedback. However, given that in many academic contexts, where daily routine is often not confined to regular hours and it is rare to find all members of a department in the same building at the same time, it can be more challenging to find opportunities for one-to-one encounters. In extreme situations, where key researchers are busy collaborating with their peers in international locations, or presenting the outcomes of their work intercontinentally, months might pass between encounters with their Head of Department. This clearly favours a distant relationship in which it may be unfeasible to find time to develop feedback skills. Nevertheless, willingness to prioritize such activity, coupled with the possibilities offered by learning technologies and social media such as Skype, can overcome even geographical remoteness.

Allocating 'quality time' for conversations is a constant challenge, given the rapidly changing nature of the economic and political environment in which universities find themselves. Dealing with short-term problems can be all-consuming, and can extinguish the energy needed to invest in high-quality, engaged relationships.

While I had always been an enthusiastic advocate of seeking and receiving regular feedback, I had rarely taken the opportunity to do so in the context of the senior leadership team of which I was part. Following the programme, I stated at the next available team meeting that I had identified four high-level objectives towards which I was working, on the basis of the feedback they had given me, in pre-programme interviews and in a 360-degree appraisal. It felt good to ask my colleagues to monitor my progress towards meeting my objectives, and opened up new channels of communication, and more constructive and engaged working relationships.

By contrast, I was once told by a participant on a programme, from a research-intensive university, that 'feedback isn't an option'. On my pursuing this, the reasons given were that the prevailing culture was one of deference to a cadre of research professors whose reputations had nourished their egos to the extent that they behaved high-handedly and did not seek feedback from departmental colleagues on their impact on others, or indeed on any other aspects of their work. Furthermore, any feedback they themselves might give to others was likely to be so intimidating that it was never asked for!

Modelling of good practice in giving and receiving feedback can be a powerful tool in the leader's repertoire. Demonstrating this in small ways works well in initiating change, and helps build a culture of trust and openness.

RESOURCE 20: INITIATING A WORKING CULTURE OF FEEDBACK

Next time you are chairing a meeting, choose a specific aspect of your behaviour on which you would like feedback. This might be an observation about how you allocate time between items on the agenda, or the way in which you include (or exclude) particular people in discussion. It may equally concern your use of influential questions, or how you build on points made in order to decide on an action. Ask a trusted colleague to make notes on your specific behaviour, and on any examples they observe of the impact of your behaviour on other people. This will provide invaluable evidence, and may surprise you, since you will more likely have focused on the content of what you've said than on its effect on others.

You may find that your colleague asks spontaneously for you to return the favour, and provide some feedback on an aspect of their own behaviour or performance. If not, you may wish to offer this. This may lead to some raised expectations from others as to the frequency and quality of feedback you give on an ongoing basis.

RESOURCE 21: GATHERING FEEDBACK ON MEETINGS

Taking an additional minute or two at the end of a meeting to gather some feedback from all participants about the process can also be helpful. This can be anonymised by asking people to write on a Post-It and paste this on the wall near the door as they leave the room. You could ask a specific question on an aspect of the meeting, such as the following.

- What were the best examples of good decision-making in this meeting?
- What changes would you suggest for next week's meeting?
- How clearly were the intended outcomes of the meeting communicated at the start?

Alternatively, you might ask participants in the meeting to evaluate it by completing sentences in response to the following prompts (these should effectively be written as instructions to the Chair of the meeting).

- STOP . . .
- START . . .
- CONTINUE . . .

This will give you an instant response as to the satisfaction levels experienced by those at the meeting, and should elicit some useful feedback around people's expectations or desires for the future. The technique will only work if you start the next meeting by reporting back on the feedback you've received, and stating what will change as a result.

CASE STUDY 8: UNIVERSITY OF CUMBRIA
Alignment and employee engagement through effective performance and professional development reviews

Background

The University of Cumbria had, for a number of years, worked on the basis of an appraisal system with annual reviews being undertaken with all permanent members of staff in the institution. However, evaluation indicated that not all areas of the university were actually complying with the review system and that modification to the existing system and related staff development was needed. In 2011 a review of the appraisal system was undertaken and relaunched as the 'performance and professional development review' (PPDR) process. The emphasis on this new process was to ensure that not only were annual PPDR reviews and interim PPDR reviews of all staff completed, but the system would facilitate regular professional conversations between reviewer and reviewee, undertaken around every four to six weeks. This would ensure the member of staff felt supported and that monitoring of the alignment of individual objectives to those of the organization could be achieved. This project was supported in part by a Small Development Project grant from the Leadership Foundation for Higher Education in 2012.

Project aims

It was recognized that the effectiveness of a performance and professional development review relied heavily on the quality of engagement with the review process itself. Work was needed to ensure that participation in the PPDR process was undertaken across the university, and a refinement of the existing process was needed to ensure and enhance the quality of engagement in the review and future planning. The intention was that an agile reflective process would be made available to facilitate continuous improvement at individual, team, departmental and organizational levels. The overall aim of the project was to identify critical factors to ensure that the performance objectives remained aligned within the increasingly dynamic and agile operating context of the university and wider sector, and to ensure that the necessary professional development was realized to support this. The benefits of the PPDR process were seen to be that it would improve and enhance performance and engage motivation, provide an agile and dynamic tool to support continuous improvement and development, and ensure staff engagement through a clear understanding of what was expected of employees as individuals and how they would be equipped to meet their performance objectives.

Staff development

A series of tailored staff development events was provided with employees at all levels and in all departments of the university. This was to ensure staff awareness of the PPDR process, what it meant for them and how they could access further information and support. The implementation of the new PPDR process involved milestones that included the following.

- First quarter
    - o completion of a staff survey on the PPDR process using the Bristol Online Survey tool
    - o focus group discussions
    - o review of the PPDR template design as a webfolio (structured multipage online document within an e-portfolio system) embedded in an existing corporate system, PebblePad. PebblePad is used by both students and staff at the university

- Second quarter
    - o data analysis of the Bristol Online Survey and further focus groups
    - o refinement of the PPDR documentation and guidance
    - o a series of reviewer workshops to support the development of the skills needed to conduct an effective PPDR, utilizing the resources available via the University of Leicester

- Third quarter
    - analysis of PPDR completion rates
    - consultation and evaluation of the evidence with the HR business managers regarding the correlation of the quality of the PPDR process and faculty/service performance
    - workshop sessions across the institution facilitated by a senior lecturer in Leadership and Organizational Development to explore the PPDR, quality of engagement in the PPDR process and the leadership and management agenda

- Fourth quarter
    - completion of an online toolkit for the project made available to the sector
    - dissemination of the project learning outcomes and outputs.

Results

The University of Cumbria has been able to ensure that 90% of its PPDR reviews have been undertaken, with the remaining 10% accounted for. There are clear examples of where good-quality professional conversations have resulted in greater equality and regularity of performance review, with greater alignment to the outputs required within the departmental area and with regard to the university. This has been achieved in part by the electronic recording mechanisms available through PebblePad, but also because of the clear links provided to the strategic plans of the university, professional bodies, performance and subject benchmarks, and the results of the National Students' Survey and other pertinent surveys.

Overall therefore each member of staff is equipped with all the information needed to ensure that the performance objectives to which he or she is working are aligned with departmental, university and national priorities. The use of a webfolio in PebblePad, reflecting on progress against objectives in professional conversations, and the ability to provide evidence electronically have enabled the monitoring mechanisms to be made efficient and effective, and every professional conversation can be recorded and data updated. The PPDR system is compulsory for every member of staff who works more than 30 hours per annum at the university. It is advised in the PPDR guidance that each member of staff has seven main objectives with a number of operational tasks associated with each of these objectives. Regular reviews are undertaken to ensure that staff are complying with the PPDR process, and this is undertaken by online surveys and HR sampling on a one-to-one basis.

Despite focused sessions and clear communications across the institution, there is still much variation in what is understood as a professional conversation. Two areas of the institution have focused heavily on professional conversations, and colleagues in those areas show a clear understanding when asked. These two areas have also shown a marked improvement in their key performance indicators since the launch of the PPDR.

The PPDR is one management tool, alongside other performance management processes, that if used correctly can facilitate an improvement in performance and provide evidence of achievement against performance benchmarks. This has been most evident in the areas that have scheduled regular sessions, on both an individual and a team basis, to discuss objectives, priorities and the necessary planning and support required to succeed, e.g. one academic colleague used the PPDR to refocus and motivate members of their team on new priorities, and an Associate Dean used professional discussions to help a colleague prioritize and plan in a new role at Faculty Management Team level.

One size does not fit all. While many colleagues have embraced PebblePad, others have continued to use the MS Word template. While the process is embedded to a significant extent, there are still discussions emerging about a bespoke system to record PPDR activity that aligns to the HR database already used.

PebblePad was offered as an option to record professional conversations and allow colleagues to revisit and reflect on their PPDR on a regular basis. Where PebblePad was already being used for other purposes in the Faculty/ Service this has worked well, with customization to add approved additional questions. In the areas that schedule regular professional conversations, members of the team have used PebblePad to keep a reflective journal on progress they are making against their objectives and will often choose to share elements of this journal with their line manager while keeping parts personal to them.

There is significant longitudinal work and learning around how the PPDR is perceived across the institution, and moving the focus from the documentation and the technology to an enduring developmental dialogue. While there are pockets of exemplary practice, there are still significant cultural challenges where the PPDR is seen as a tick-box exercise done once a year for compliance rather than development. In many cases, these are the same areas that exhibit poor performance and require focused and targeted professional development in, for example, digital literacy.

Feedback about the PPDR process has also underlined the vital role managers play in connecting the conversations as recorded to co-ordinated developmental planning.

Conclusion

The full implementation of the new PPDR process at the University of Cumbria has yet to be completed. Nevertheless, there are clear signs of the effectiveness of the mechanism in terms both of the take-up from staff and of the achievement and alignment of objectives within the university.

Questions

1   How does your institution facilitate an individual achieving their PPDR targets?
2   How does your institution align an individual's targets with the strategic goals of the organization?

Case study developed by Alice Helm-Alabaster, University of Cumbria, and Professor Dawn Forman.

Learning from feedback approaches
Building a virtuous cycle of constructive criticism

While there may some initial discomfort when you begin to challenge established conventions, resist the temptation to feel that you tried it once, and it didn't work. Persistence will lead to improved practice, and as people become accustomed to using the language of feedback, expectations (and performance) will increase.

The model of Situation–Behaviour–Impact, developed by the Center for Creative Leadership (King and Santana, 2010), helps in providing feedback that is genuinely based on evidence, rather than on judgement of others' personalities, appearance or other aspects that they can do little to change. King and Santana report that:

> Many of the managers who attend our programs are uncomfortable with providing feedback to others, particularly negative feedback. Most do not feel highly skilled in this practice, and they lack models or tools to help them provide developmental feedback to others or receive it themselves.
>
> (2010: 112–13)

The model works by encouraging its users to develop skills in observation, recording evidence, and using this evidence to raise awareness – and encourage changes of behaviour – in others. It helps to avoid a natural tendency to make such comments as 'I thought you were rather negative in that meeting'. By establishing a very specific instance in a particular setting, and then citing a concrete example of the behaviour used by a given individual, this approach enables the other party to recall the cognitive and emotional state in which they found themselves. It also provides a backdrop for what you observed of the impact of the other person's behaviour (often verbal, but sometimes a bodily gesture, facial expression or something connected to the tone or register of an utterance) on either yourself or others involved in the situation.

Those who become skilled in using this model are able to identify instances in which the other party is more likely to have been quite unaware of the impact of their actions on others, often as a result of being so deeply absorbed in the content of a task or message that they failed to pick up on signals being given to them by those around them. The feedback that is given as a result can lead to significant insight, and can fuel the will to change behaviours and relationships. Acquiring the skills needed can therefore prove to be an invaluable investment of time and effort.

RESOURCE 22: MAKING FEEDBACK SPECIFIC

The feedback conversation is likely to be most successful if it focuses on specific examples of evidence of behaviour and language, and the directly observed impact of these instances on others involved.

Begin practising by identifying specific instances of behaviour about which you could usefully provide feedback. Make a list of four or five colleagues who might benefit from your feedback. For each colleague, think of three instances in the recent past (preferably the last week, if possible) that were significant. Then, for each example you have identified, note the exact behaviour you observed (this may include quoting some of the language you heard), and – most importantly – the impact it had.

How difficult was this task? It's unlikely that you will readily bring examples to mind, unless you are regularly in the practice of gathering evidence to use in feedback. You may find it tough to recall enough details of a situation in which you were deeply involved yourself. It does take practice – and is likely to be worth the effort!

The next step is to make use of the evidence you have built up. There may be a natural context in which to offer the feedback. If not, you may need to set up a situation carefully. The first time you try using this, it may be helpful to choose a single example, and to relate this to a setting that you need to discuss in any case. This might be a particular project, task or relationship about which you have already agreed to talk.

You will need to make a decision about the balance between positive and negative feedback – focusing entirely on one to the exclusion of others is likely to result in sceptical or cynical responses.

TIP: You may find that the person you are feeding back to is also able to offer feedback to you, and you may wish to seek this first. This will build rapport, and help to smooth channels of communication.

CASE STUDY 9: UNIVERSITY OF BRISTOL
Faculty restructuring to secure a stronger research performance

Background

Having worked in the aerospace industry prior to starting at the University of Bristol and having had 18 years' experience at the university prior to being appointed Dean of Faculty, a newly appointed Dean of Engineering was very clear about both the external environmental changes that were impacting on the university, particularly those of a financial nature, and the changes that were needed within the university to make it more effective and efficient for the future. In 2009, therefore, the new Dean was clear in his own mind that he had to articulate the need for change, win the hearts and minds of staff within his faculty and streamline systems and processes to enable the faculty to pursue its aspiration to continue to be in the top three for research in the UK and the top five internationally. This was to be achieved while maintaining the consistently high performance in the Undergraduate National Student Survey and the proven employability of graduate students.

While this aspiration was clear in the mind of the incoming Dean, the success of the faculty hitherto meant that the internal culture was one where the need for change was not apparent to all staff. The faculty was indeed deemed to be relatively successful. It was clear that any need for change would have to be clearly articulated and demonstrably thought through, and would have to draw on a clear evidence base that would be appreciated by both the academic and support staff. At the same time, the university itself also felt the need for considerable change, but consideration of how and when this would be undertaken was not apparent.

Providing an evidence base

Working with a small team, the Dean gathered an evidence base for the need for change. This included data reviews, both internally and through comparisons with other universities, staff interviews and the identification of good practice and also areas of weakness. The aspects that were identified as needing to change included:

- the diversity of the teaching
- the duplication of teaching and systems
- the multiple departmental research groups
- a more streamlined approach to costing processes to facilitate bidding for and winning grants
- clear recognition of squeezed physical and financial resources

- more resilient support structures based on the 'one task, one place' philosophy
- clear honing of the schools and support structures in the two buildings of the faculty.

Once this evidence had been gathered, consultants were appointed with a very clear steer to review the evidence, to ensure that comparisons with other universities were appropriately benchmarked, taking account of external environmental factors, and to position the faculty for future success.

A consultation document was derived in April 2009, articulating the results of this evidence-gathering and providing a clear academic rationale for undertaking the change (summary provided in the annex below). This clear rationale was extremely important in winning the hearts and minds of staff, many of whom gave the impression that this might well be 'the end of the world as they knew it', and some of whom were not only sceptical but also disruptive towards any moves in the new direction.

The rationale for the change was, therefore, made clear and compelling – the faculty needed to develop a way of working that:

1   allowed them to build large-scale research groups that had an international presence
2   allowed them to continue to deliver excellent taught programmes that attracted high-quality students but were simpler to run
3   allowed them to rationalize the processes and structure in order to become both more resilient and more agile.

Consultation and communication

- A clear process of consultation was developed.
- The need for change was clearly articulated.
- Discussion fora were formulated.
- Question and answer sessions were not only made available in face to face meetings but also articulated within documentation that was widely circulated.
- Away days were held.
- Newsletters were constructed and widely distributed on a regular basis.
- Timetable outlines for the changes needed by when and who was responsible were clearly articulated.

Clear throughout the process was that the main agenda was not to lose staff but to ensure that systems and processes were in place that would support the faculty for the future and enable increased income to be derived with high-quality provision in terms of both teaching and research.

The resulting structure

The refined faculty structure had two academic schools, each based within its own building. Students and staff therefore had one location to go to associated with their school and with their building. This streamlined the structures and functions for the undergraduate provision.

A graduate school was developed to ensure that units that had been duplicates in their offering were streamlined, such that units with the same name were no longer being taught to fewer than eight students but some now had 40 students within their provision.

The four research units that had existed within the faculty were brought together. This, together with supporting administrative structures, ensured more effective and streamlined bidding and costing processes and better record keeping. The number of committees and their scheduling was also reviewed and streamlined.

The results

While it is too early to predict an increase in research quality, significant changes have been seen that include:

- 30% increase in income to the faculty
- 50% reduction in the number of committees
- a decrease of staff by 10, owing to natural wastage
- clear identification with the faculty and university's overall aims
- a rolling out of the restructuring that occurred within the faculty is now taking place in the rest of the university.

Lessons learnt

As the Dean reflects on the process, there are some key lessons he learnt along the journey that relate largely to communication with stakeholders.

- Firstly he assumed autonomy and, with hindsight, should have ensured that senior management was supportive at every stage of the restructuring process. Part-way through the process, the implications for the rest of the university were made apparent and the restructuring of his faculty had to be put on hold while the university could consider the wider implications. Therefore if he were starting again he would manage upwards more effectively.
- He would ensure that each stage was signed off by the faculty board, thereby officially gaining support of the staff.
- He would ensure that the immediate team taking this process forward would hold and maintain the same values and messages so that they

- could be articulated clearly and in a consistent way to all staff within the faculty.
- He would consider a more differentiated communication process to ensure that stakeholders were appropriately informed.

As the new Dean he was struck by the loneliness of the position – a clear feeling at times that, if he was not able to make a success of this change and take people with him, he would need to stand down from the role. However, such was the success that, as from September 2011, the Dean became Pro-Vice Chancellor (Education) at the University of Bristol.

Questions

1   How effective and efficient are the systems and processes within your area? Does duplication exist and could this be more effectively streamlined?
2   Which key stakeholder groups need to be communicated with as change takes place within your organization?
3   Do you feel isolated in your leadership role? What support mechanisms can you build in for the future?

Case study developed by Professor N.A.J. Lieven, Pro-Vice Chancellor Education, University of Bristol and Professor Dawn Forman.

Annex

EF21 Academic Vision

As the university moves from 42 departments to 22 schools and we become two schools in Engineering, I thought it would be helpful to remind everyone of the rationale for doing this and to restate the academic vision. Administratively, we can all see why more robust common systems are of benefit to everyone, students and staff alike. Academically, EF21 similarly must put us in a better place – at all levels. The aspiration to be in the top five in the UK now seems unambitious given our success in the Research Assessment Exercise and in developing large-scale Centres for Doctoral Training, our consistently high performance in the undergraduate National Student Survey and the proven employability of our graduates. We should now aim to be in the top three in the UK and in the top five internationally, and we will achieve our vision as follows.

Undergraduate education

- We will attract the very best students (AAA+) and educate them to be the leaders of their generation by demonstrating flair and individuality.

- We will distinguish ourselves from our competitors through discipline-focused education, so that we attract students with outstanding intake grades who are highly motivated in their discipline.
- We will encourage students, while being grounded within a discipline, to flourish and to develop an individual excellence that marks them out from their peers.

Postgraduate education

- We will attract the best research students by providing an outstanding educational environment through the strengths of our research groups and the capacity of our Centres for Doctoral Training and the new Graduate School to provide fully integrated skills development.
- We will offer specialist advanced education (such as Internet Technologies with Security, or Advanced Microelectronic Systems Engineering) that is shaped by our research strengths but is also linked through to professional need.
- We will offer broadly based postgraduate programmes (such as Computer Science, Water and Environmental Management, or Advanced Mechanical Engineering) to attract excellent students who wish to acquire new knowledge and skills or augment a first degree.

Research

- We will have Research Groups that are internationally known as THE centres of knowledge and that will be the first choice of destination for industry, permanent and visiting scholars, EU programme consortia and the research councils.
- We will be known for our open scientific approach to collaboration and partnership.
- We will be distinguished by our ability to deliver multidisciplinary research focused on the grand societal challenges that are underpinned by strong disciplines.

Coaching conversations
The stuff of every corridor

When I became a Head of Department, I prided myself on having an 'open door' policy, meaning that colleagues who felt the need to raise issues could feel free to do so unless I was in a scheduled meeting or appointment. People used this in different ways. Worriers sought to have weight lifted from their shoulders. Others unloaded fears and anxieties. Chancers saw opportunities to seek funding and favours. Relatively few of these spontaneous encounters had a character that could be described as developmental, because of the way I handled them. I exuded a certain sense of calm, and sometimes helped my colleagues to find solutions to problems, but often absorbed the stress that others carried in with them. Feedback on my approach was vaguely positive, but it was only some years later than I realized how many opportunities I had missed to engage my colleagues more deeply.

What would have contributed enormously to deeper conversations, and undoubtedly to better outcomes for individuals and our department, would have been to approach them using a coaching style.

Whitmore (1992) developed a widely adopted model for structuring a coaching conversation in a way that not only focuses on outcomes, but also positions responsibility for decisions and actions firmly with the 'coachee' rather than with the 'coach'/manager. Furthermore, it provides a sense of direction in a conversation that moves towards a clear conclusion, and thus avoids the sensation of going round in repeating circles.

Coaching conversations fit well into departmental cultures that embody rising spirals of expectations and, once embedded, can become compelling. If you find yourself always in the role of coach, and never have the opportunity to be at the 'other side' of the conversation, it would be worth thinking about how you might find a colleague – either in or beyond your department – who can in turn coach you. Responding to challenging questions that are put to you by a skilled coach can provide powerful insights, not only into the decisions and actions to which you yourself might wish to commit, but also into how to improve your practice in coaching conversations.

There are some compelling examples in the research of coaching cultures permeating entire educational institutions, particularly in the schools sector. Lofthouse et al. highlight examples from their research which show that:

> where coaching is systematically built into the [Continuing Professional Development] strategy and time allocated to it (within both the core timetable and directed time) coaching was found to flourish. This involved the strategic leadership of coaching by the [Senior Leadership Team] within the overall CPD strategy . . . An important message . . . is that coaching can support teachers who genuinely wish to improve to develop their practice, and can be used to improve teaching and learning across the school as a whole.
>
> (2010: 16–18)

Here, the role of leaders in establishing the climate in which coaching conversations thrive was seen as critical to success. The stronger the model of collaborative engagement demonstrated by teams of senior leaders, the greater are the chances of success across the wider organization.

Enticing as these examples are, it is worth bearing in mind that coaching conversations do not have to take place in relatively lengthy discussions; short conversations in informal settings can reinforce the developmental role you have as a leader, and enable others to re-energize with remarkable rapidity. As you develop your repertoire of skills in coaching conversations, you will be able to tune in more rapidly to the extent to which different individuals respond more fully to cognitively driven (Head) or affectively oriented (Heart) questions. However, responding fully does not necessarily equate to the amount of talking they might do. Talking can often belie full processing of ideas or feelings. You are also likely to find yourself sensing the amount of challenge or stretch you notice in your coachee, and in this way, apparent discomfort can be an indicator of the existence of appropriate conditions for learning.

One of the key principles to bear in mind when engaging in coaching conversations is that the skills required are quite distinct from those traditionally associated with didactic teaching. Any assumption that the coach holds the solution to the coachee's problems, or that the coach may ask questions to which she already knows the answer, must be set aside. For a coaching relationship to work, it is essential that the coach overcomes any notion of demonstrating her own prowess, and only asks questions where the answer is yet to be determined. The conversation must, in other words, be fuelled by authentic curiosity and inquiry-mindedness.

The GROW model advocated by Whitmore (1992) provides a staged framework for sequencing a coaching conversation. It enables coachees to work towards establishing the actions they are prepared to commit to taking in order to resolve their own problems.

Using four stages to sequence a conversation, the coach initially questions the coachee about the Goals that the coachee would like to achieve, and thus builds a picture of what success looks like for the individual. The second stage focuses on the Reality of the current situation, including an understanding of what has been achieved to date. The third stage considers Options for potential action, and provides an opportunity to generate new ideas and to challenge what appear to be fixed assumptions. Finally, coach and coachee establish what is the coachee's Will – what actions will she actually take, and what support is needed?

CASE STUDY 10: UNIVERSITY OF HERTFORDSHIRE
Leading through coaching

Background

The University of Hertfordshire has developed a strong, collaborative internal relationship between the School of Education and the Human Resources Development team. It has also been involved in a number of projects with the UK Leadership Foundation for Higher Education.

Leading through Coaching was commissioned by Kevin Flinn, Head of Leadership and Organisational Development at the University of Hertfordshire, as an integral part of the Responding to the Challenges of Leading programme and a catalyst for the development of a coaching culture within the University (Hawkins and Smith, 2011; Forman et al., 2013). This was seen as necessary to ensure the development of a leadership culture that aligned with the university's values and that enabled staff from across the university to develop appropriate leadership and coaching skills.

The initiative and implementation

The School of Education (SoE) had been running professional development programmes for experienced teachers for many years and Sally Graham, who had been the programme director for this area and who was an experienced coach, was asked to build on this experience to develop a coaching programme that would lead to Master's degree credits for staff within the university. The range of staff involved would include both very senior leaders and managers and those new to these roles in academic, professional and technical contexts. The diversity of staff was seen to be an advantage to the university in relation to developing a shared culture, and beneficial to course participants who could gain from understanding a wide range of perspectives. Participants from the first cohort reported that this diversity had indeed deepened their understanding of the wider context of the university, and the different ways leadership was enacted.

The design of the programme, built on Sally's experience of developing teacher education programmes and on her knowledge of coaching and current coaching provision, was supported by research accessed through the UK Leadership Foundation for Higher Education. The aims of the programme were: to develop knowledge and skills in the field of coaching and mentoring; to deepen understanding of the role of coaching and mentoring in facilitating the learning of others; to identify how coaching and mentoring can facilitate leadership development; and to show how those skills can be used in leadership roles.

An initial cohort of 24 university staff members undertook the programme, and following its success it was decided to continue to make this available to university staff but also to open the campus-based programme to external participants and to develop an online route.

Within the programme the 3-D model (Graham et al., 2012) was used to support participants' reflection on practice and the development of their coaching skills. Participants coached a member of staff from the wider university and used the 3-D model (see Figure 5.1) to guide their practice. This model was also related to participants' own leadership in their professional contexts and they collected, shared and analysed significant moments or critical incidents within their practice to identify developing insights and changes of approach. The use made of the model is shown in Figure 5.2.

The eight-day programme was divided into two sections. During the first four days participants were supported to develop relationship coaching skills that were then used in coaching a member of staff in the university

Figure 5.1 The 3-D model

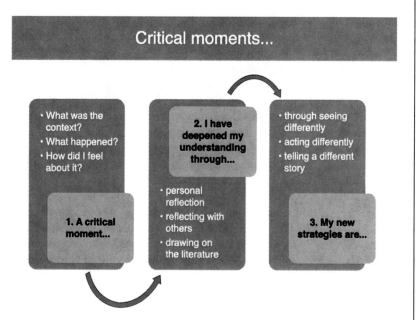

Figure 5.2 Application of the 3-D model in coaching conversations

and in their leadership practice. During this time, and between the two sets of four days, the participants were asked to construct a learning journal in which they reflected on 'critical moments' in their coaching conversations with their coachee and with colleagues in formal and informal meetings (de Haan and Blass, 2007). The key focus was on developing listening skills and using an approach that would encourage the coachee or colleague to work on their issues through the use of coaching questions. We identified Relational Coaching as one style of coaching that might offer a central vehicle for developing an effective peer coaching culture within higher education. Relational in this context means 'acknowledging the inherently mutual nature of all social process', and prioritizing 'the importance of the co-created, "here-and-now" relationship as the central vehicle for development and transformation' (Critchley, 2010).

During the second four days participants explored approaches to coaching groups and a co-coaching model, again developed from de Haan and Blass's work. This included looking at different ways of running meetings, facilitating the use of listening skills in group settings, and approaching issues through appreciative enquiry and action research. The aim was that participants would develop the facility to use peer coaching as the default approach for the practice of leadership and management. As an outcome of a positive review of the programme, it is now being offered across the university to a second cohort and is being developed into a Master's programme offered externally and in an online format. Further requests have been made by university staff members for more people-led coaching skills, more supervision skills and more opportunities to network both within and outside the university with regard to implementing coaching within the day-to-day context. Further developments also include funding from the Leadership Foundation for Higher Education to lead a project exploring the development of coaching in Higher Education with two other universities – Anglia Ruskin and Brighton.

Evaluation

The programme was evaluated using 30-minute interviews with each participant. The feedback identified significant changes to thinking and practice made by participants, for example:

> My new-found coaching skills help in relationships with the [name] team who can be a bit tricky at times.

> I have more awareness around people, the things they do, the way they work. Having that awareness about things . . . It has broadened my whole thinking.

> On a professional level when I am holding team meetings, I deal with things differently now. I ask how staff are, how they are feeling. How I approach and manage my colleagues is completely different. I now ask . . . have you been ok with that? Have you got any concerns? Before the course I was always very task-oriented.

Conclusion

While the University of Hertfordshire is still in its initial stages of developing a coaching culture (Clutterbuck and Megginson, 2006; Forman et al., 2013) and approach to leadership, there have already been signs that this type of professional development can enhance the skills of managers and leaders within the university. The Human Resource Development Team is seeking to implement this way of managing and leading within the university, and is evaluating the impact of this programme in contributing to changes in practice. Such is the success of this programme to date that other universities are already looking to implement a similar model within their institutions.

Questions

1   Does your organization have a coaching culture?
2   Do you think that a programme to facilitate managers to be coaches would be beneficial to achieving the goals of the organization?

Case study developed by Professor Dawn Forman and Sally Graham, University of Hertfordshire.

6 Working in partnerships

Higher education and public value

Influencing challenges
Beyond institutional boundaries

Research into the work of those responsible for building collaborative external partnerships for universities points to the importance of high-order influencing skills, together with a wide range of other capabilities, including those of boundary-spanning, tolerance of uncertainty, willingness to embrace complexity, and ability to establish norms for collaborative working (Wagstaff, 2013).

The desired outcomes of effective external influencing are many and varied, and include, for instance:

- gaining capital investment for civic projects involving other services such as museums, theatres or sports organizations;
- sharing core infrastructure services, such as public transportation or car parking;
- building understanding in order to create social, cultural or commercial partnerships of mutual benefit to all participants;
- contributing to leadership of place.

Effective leaders in higher education institutions are likely to have built a repertoire of successful influencing skills that work inside their universities and colleges. These might include the ability to present powerful rational arguments that are articulated within theoretically informed intellectual frameworks. They may also apply a capacity for building conversational bridges that enable others to express their own expectations, hopes and fears, and in doing so, increasing the chances of successful influencing outcomes.

In practice, these will not necessarily translate directly into other organizational cultures, and leaders engaging beyond institutional boundaries will need to find ways of testing out their assumptions. In gauging the responses of partners to their approaches, university leaders will acquire a sense of what is likely to work most successfully in generating trust and securing engagement.

Leaders who can work successfully across boundaries are likely to turn potential barriers into frontiers of exploration. As expressed by Ernst et al. (2010), this example of leadership at work is represented by the difference between stifled creativity and human talent on one hand, and breakthrough thinking and results on the other. Ernst et al. outline a range of techniques and approaches that can be used to span various categories of boundaries, including those defined by geography, human diversity, functional and organisational silos and ring-fences, and by rank, authority and power.

Some of these approaches may lend themselves better to working across internal boundaries, while others will be more applicable to external barriers. Partnerships with other organizations can be fraught with difficulties due to differences between partners as to the fluidity (or otherwise) of internal structures. While it is easy to cite a model approach to increasing the extent of genuine collaboration or interdependence, in practice there are likely to be challenges arising from organizational cultural differences in how people speak and act.

Here is a selection of approaches suggested by Ernst et al. (2010), with brief commentaries as to implications for using each of them in practice.

In attempting to bring together different organizations – for instance, in a collaborative project – where each has a unique role to contribute, and the sum total is a larger whole (presumably greater than the sum of the parts), Ernst et al. outline a 'weaving' approach. This can be boosted by practices of:

- encouraging open, challenging debate within the partnership, but acting as one once agreement is reached. This requires tremendous collective will, backed by rigorous processes of monitoring and feedback. It is clearly essential to ensure that consent is genuine, whole-hearted and constructive once reached, and this implies giving close attention to how the internal debate process is chaired or facilitated. This cannot be tokenistic, but must use challenging open questions that surface political and emotional issues. If there remains any unspoken business, this will clearly impair genuine buy-in. Using time in meetings to do this rather than 'business as usual' may elicit some initial resistance, but should ultimately prove to be a worthwhile investment.
- facilitating flexible membership of project teams, changing the mix between partner organizations as needs arise. Real partnerships only grow when collaborative expertise is shared, and a different set of outcomes achieved from what would otherwise have been the case for individual constituent partners. Dividing up activities within existing boundaries will therefore not bring full partnership benefits to fruition, so exchanging and moving around staff appears attractive in terms of shared learning and capacity-building. It may lead to risks emerging, as well as opportunities. As the partner organizations cross-fertilize, distinct working cultures may be threatened. Ultimately, the chances of alliances and even mergers arising might increase. Applying an 'appreciative inquiry' approach to managing colleagues who are boundary spanners in this way should ensure a focus on learning, rather than on obsession with territorialism.

When a partnership leads to the creation of a new organization in which people need to work inside a newly defined boundary that is larger than what individuals have previously known, Ernst et al. talk about 'mobilizing' approaches. Practices that help to create a new common sense of purpose include the following.

- 'Skip level meetings': here middle leaders play a crucial role as the organizational glue by bringing together their (newly configured) direct reports with the person to whom the middle manager reports. The format used is that of a 'summit meeting' conversation about goals and strategy for the new organization. This clearly erodes concerns that may have been expressed initially. However, there is a risk that if undertaken only once, with minimal follow-up feedback and action, the exercise will be viewed cynically as a token act. If such meetings are planned regularly as part of a systemic effort to create a boundary-less culture, their full potential is much more likely to be realized.
- Using narrative to bring alive the purpose and identity of the new organization. In a study of how senior leaders engage their staff across a wide range of organizations in different sectors, Hockey and Ley (2010) identified a single common factor in the practice of successful leaders – their ability to harness the power of narrative. Telling stories and building vivid pictures of what success looks like – and similarly how dramatic the consequences of failure might be – can be highly influential in moving people towards desired organizational goals. In a newly formed organization, developing a narrative that 'sticks', in that people feel impelled to carve out opportunities to tell it to others, can provide a fast and effective means to crossing what might previously have been seen as boundaries. There are examples of universities that experienced merger many years in the past, but where the norms and subcultures of predecessor institutions are still jealously guarded. The mobilizing approaches might have been used to good effect in these contexts. However, a major drawback around narratives centres on the discomfort often felt by leaders when they perceive that they are not good at the language and behaviours that are required, and that introducing storytelling into their repertoire would immediately be detected by colleagues as deeply inauthentic. The lower the degree of emotional intelligence in an organization, the more challenging it may be to use narrative successfully.

Ernst et al.'s category of 'reflecting' approaches should appeal to those in educational institutions that consider themselves to be learning organizations. This is fundamentally about sharing insights and developing a sense of inquiry across separate organizational boundaries. The Leadership Foundation has developed a methodology within some of its programmes that draws on this concept. Organizations that are not higher education institutions (and thus offer some alternative cultural environments to those with which participants are familiar) open themselves up to a collaborative inquiry by a group of up to 20 university leaders, and set the group a challenge question concerning aspects of strategy. As long as the question is one to which the host organization is genuinely open to wanting to think about a set of responses, there is a strong sense of mutual learning (and plenty of opportunity for leadership to emerge from within the visiting group). Ernst et al. suggest the following.

- Cross-group inquiries in which participants build a sense of mastery of asking powerful questions. Just as action learning provides a context in which participants develop greater awareness and skill as to which questions work best in triggering challenge and insight, so this form of collaborative enquiry affords rich practice opportunities. Sensitivity is needed to ensure that questions do not cause offence by implying superiority or greater expertise on the part of the questioner. As with any aspect of leadership in performance, practice leads to improvement.
- Cross-shadow groups, which allow for individual members from different partner organizations to spend short periods (half a day is suggested) observing one another in their respective contexts, and subsequently share insights and learning. This practice can be strengthened by individual participants improving their ability to write up what they have observed, prior to having a feedback conversation.

Finally, Ernst et al.'s category of 'connecting' will be familiar to all who work in universities, given its focus on networks, conferences and brokered meetings – all of which are the lifeblood of professional services communities in higher education, and of academic disciplines.

Building partnerships and collaborations

In mapping the landscape of partnerships and collaborations in higher education, Wagstaff (2013) sets out a gamut of forms and motivations that inform institutions' practice. These include alliances and mergers between institutions themselves, partnerships established as vehicles for transnational education, commercial ventures and arrangements for rationalizing provision of back-office functions.

While considerable effort has been put into rationalization of services provided by public bodies (particularly city councils and other local authorities), universities seem to have been slower at being able to engage with shared services. In the UK, national review bodies have produced detailed recommendations in pursuit of increased efficiency and modernization, such as the Diamond Review (Universities UK, 2011). Yet, according to experts in shared services elsewhere in the education sector (in schools and further education institutions), higher education institutions have developed little maturity in their outlook and practices concerning such services. Universities, it is claimed, are happy to share services as long as they themselves are providing them, and others are contracted to paying them. This willingness to be lead partners in collaborations, but less so to be more junior players in give-and-take relationships, has arguably led to missed strategic opportunities. It has possibly also contributed to underdevelopment of partnership-working skills among higher education leaders.

Goddard (2009) argues passionately for the contribution that universities can make to their cities and regions, and articulates in some detail the tasks that need to be undertaken in order to create the requisite vehicles for partnership. More recently, the UK government reinforced its message that universities are 'the driving force behind our increasingly high-tech, knowledge-based economy' (Cabinet Office, 2013).

Some helpful tools are available to enable universities to determine their readiness for engaging in partnership activity, and others exist to help them sharpen their skills in order to make engagement successful.

Ironically, just as universities were building the capabilities needed to contribute successfully to the leadership of place, the global economic crisis occurred, and one of the earliest victims was public funding to support partnerships in communities. Nevertheless, collaborative work has continued, and partnerships have had to find new ways to sustain themselves. In some ways, attention did not necessarily need to be paid carefully to the processes and cultures of partnership, as long as money was flowing. Paucity of funding has arguably forced more effective collaboration.

Work at the University of Birmingham/Homes & Communities Agency (2011) has identified five core behaviours that are critical to leadership of place (2011: 16–17). The core behaviours are named and characterized in the leadership roles of Challenger, Influencer, Balancer, Questioner and Learner. These are particularly interesting in that in some ways they run counter to the prevailing corporate behaviours one might expect to find amongst fairly senior leaders in higher education. Perhaps the most challenging aspects are those concerning the willingness to set aside the immediate needs of one's own institution:

> Leaders of place need to be able to relate to others and identify their own individual drivers as distinct from the drivers of the organisations who sent them.
>
> (2011:16)

This raises some interesting risks and dilemmas not only for the individuals concerned, but also for those to whom they report, and those they manage within their universities. A new sense of tolerance of ambiguity and uncertainty is called for, along with a deeper sense of trust placed in those who navigate their institutions through new landscapes of local and regional partnerships. At the same time, it is crucial to apply empathy to one's work in leadership of place, in order to understand and respond to the needs of others.

There are several other aspects of the five core behaviours that bear strong resemblance to the characteristics of the 'learning leader' we have considered earlier in this book. As might be expected, those who are able to develop and nurture cultures of participation, enquiry and engagement are also likely to bring strengths to working in partnership and collaboration.

The Challenger, for instance, is able to 'challenge the prevailing culture and develop a mutually supportive system' (ibid.). Questioner behaviours are the antithesis of command-and-control approaches, in that they do not imply that leaders can provide solutions, but rather that they 'go in with questions which will help shape a bespoke solution through conversation and innovation' (ibid.).

Alongside the Questioner, the Learner behaviours sit comfortably. Of particular importance is the ability to realize the potential for learning from failure, rather than solely from so-called best practice. Talking openly and widely about practice is likely to pay dividends, particularly in times of uncertainty. Wagstaff raises some challenging questions about institutional capacity for learning:

> Does [the institution] identify lessons and then apply them to other partnership situations? Does it use those lessons to inform whether it should go into future partnerships and if so how, why and when? Is it able to articulate individual and organisational competency in the area and expedite future relationships more effectively? Does the organisation reflect on how it is changed by being in partnership and what individual partnerships are contributing to its own evolving ecology? . . . the indications are that this does not take place in any conscious or systematised way.
>
> (2013: 17)

Using some of the tools we have presented in previous chapters should help to create an appropriate climate in which people feel safe to divulge their own experiences, whether or not the outcomes were successful.

All the practices highlighted in this chapter are critical to the realization of the concept of the public value that is provided by higher education in terms of social and cultural capital at least as much as in the importance of their contribution to the economy and to employment.

This concept acquires greater urgency if we take account of the picture outlined by Mulgan (2010) in his identification of the 'relational state'. Mulgan argues that the era of 'production' of public services has become redundant, and with it the associated processes of setting targets 'centred around performance, delivery, and doing things to or for people' (2010: 2). In doing so, he sweeps aside the notions of choice and competition, and of efficiency in 'transforming inputs of money into measurable outputs' (2010: 2).

Instead, he suggests the prevailing importance of public organizations addressing the quality of their relationships with those they serve. This implies a very different character of organizational life, in which subjective measures (such as those based on emotional perceptions and responses) become predominant. Front-end behaviours take on considerably greater importance than back-room operations, since these are likely to be geared towards prompting feedback and communicating organizational responses to such feedback.

In Mulgan's vision, notions of co-creation and co-production 'become more formalised' (2010: 3), and working through partnerships (without always being a dominant player) takes on greater significance.

The longer-term implications of such new models of public service are highly significant for those running universities, in terms of the sustainability of our institutions and the communities in which they are located, and also of the leadership and working cultures that will be required. These are the substance of the final chapter.

CASE STUDY 11: THE UNIVERSITY OF SHEFFIELD AND SHEFFIELD HALLAM UNIVERSITY
Collaboration Sheffield: transformational change with an old and new university in the same city

Background

Collaboration Sheffield was proposed by two incoming Vice-Chancellors in order to bring together complementary academic areas to provide a unique and rounded educational/research offer for the city/region and to support social and economic transformation directly. External factors such as change in government and more focus on Local Enterprise Partnerships also prompted this change. This project was intended to help the universities lead and contribute to policy development in areas of greatest socio-economic need for the city/region. Hence, four 'strands' of activity (Education, Healthcare, Digital and Knowledge Transfer) have been selected for development. Both Vice-Chancellors believe that:

- the sum of the individual strands is likely to be stronger than the individual academic parts if transformation were sought;
- this project should seek to achieve academic and financial dividends;
- an activity of this nature will also preserve the identity and heritage of two distinct universities (i.e. not lead to merger) whilst demonstrating the value of effective collaboration to the region and to an extent managing the expectations of partners and stakeholders and focusing the deployment of resources in the city region through joint consultation and collaboration.

The challenges

(i) Corporate challenges

In the initial stages of the project, effort was placed on defining the nature of the project and establishing effective governance structures in which the Vice Chancellors held visible and effective leadership roles. This has helped to align the differing corporate cultures and provide a common framework for the operation of the project. Most importantly, this provided a clear indication from the Vice-Chancellors that academic transformation was critical to the success of this project.

(ii) Academic challenges

It has been essential to appoint joint project leaders (one from each university) and to provide time for team building and debate (as well as external professional facilitation to ensure progress and independent advice on potential transformation). Key aspects of this have included: overcoming local histories; rethinking traditional academic approaches; rethinking traditional collaborative approaches (i.e. moving from competition to partnership); establishing team-building/trust/rapport; understanding the need for the project; overcoming suspicion about a merger; and seeking transformational activity.

(iii) External challenges

The delivery of the project was affected by a change of government and fundamental structural changes in significant sectors, nationally in HE, Education and Health and regionally with the formation of the City region-focused governance structure, the Local Enterprise Partnerships (LEPs).

Impact on the curriculum

Collaboration to develop new approaches to teaching

Significant impact on the student body and the curriculum are areas that were not strongly anticipated in the original proposal in 2010. However work in inter-professional education has brought together social work students with those in health and medicine across institutional boundaries to develop specially created distance learning materials based on an authentic patient story that forms a basis for inter-professional working groups across the universities. This and the joint work on CPD for teachers and the potential of ICT in education has prompted consideration of jointly accredited modules, an emerging theme in the Education and Health strands that is likely to prompt the two strands to work together to consider the challenges and benefits of joint accreditation for the two institutions.

Stakeholder engagement

In order to bring about transformations that have an impact on city/regional policy, it is recognized by all strands that it will be essential to engage stakeholders in discussions at an early stage. However, all strands concluded through their discussions that having a tangible 'offer' is critical to the successful engagement of stakeholders, and all have opted to take this forward later in the project.

Transformation and new approaches

Phase 1 of the project provided time and structured debate on what might be achieved and what might be transformational. Initial proposals were put forward to the Vice-Chancellors and, at the end of this phase, selected projects were approved. These are now being developed in Phase 2 to become enduring and transformational developments, and include the following.

- **Education** – an Education/Strategy Policy Forum; a joint ICT consultancy venture.
- **Digital** – a living lab for Sheffield to underpin a 'smart cities' approach to regional development; a joint digital healthcare technologies group.
- **Healthcare** – a Medicine and Health Strategic Forum; a joint Sheffield Institute for Healthcare Technologies; and training for health leaders in the university and NHS.
- **Knowledge Transfer** – joint engagement in Local Area Partnership, Technology Innovation Centre and Regional Growth Hub proposals and a revised focus on a joint approach to innovation support.

Collaboration Sheffield has brought together colleagues, many of whom had no history of working with each other – particularly the case in Digital and Education – to identify priorities and jointly engage with stakeholders.

Impact on investment by HEFCE has:

- developed 13 substantive projects; four each in Education, Health and Digital, and one in KT. These include consultative groups, interventions addressing stakeholder priorities, curriculum development and student engagement;
- created a legacy of an ongoing set of activities, a platform for further development and a wealth of lessons learned and insight based on two and a half years of experience;
- moved the relationships of the two universities from informal interaction to structured collaboration in targeted sectors, and paved the way for joint working in other sectors and collaboration at a strategic, institutional level;
- created a joint and structured dialogue with stakeholders in the region leading to coordinated interventions;
- mobilized a significant resource through the engagement of the two VCs, securing the commitment of a team of eight senior leads across four strands of activity supported by four members of a central team, and engaged around 40 members of staff in meaningful project delivery.

Learning to date

Key learning points to date include:

- joint VC leadership and high-profile presence are essential to securing change;
- stimulation of the academic ideas needs strong academic input and leadership – and should be complemented by high-quality support. The key issues of sustainability, academic and financial dividends and transformation need to be developed more carefully in Phase 2;
- a high-quality external facilitator can act as a catalyst;

- academic teams need space and time for debate but will also need a timeframe by which debate should be concluded;
- this approach has been beneficial not only to the two institutions but to the wider organizations and public of Sheffield.

Questions

1   What are the advantages and disadvantages of such strategic partnerships in the present economic climate?
2   What factors would you consider for a collaborative partnership for research?
3   How would you monitor the effectiveness of such a collaboration?

Case study developed by Professor Michael Smith, Sheffield Hallam University, and Dr Claire Baines, University of Sheffield.

Public value
Concept and practice

As universities focused increasingly during the 2000s on running themselves as complex and effective businesses, they ran the risk of alienating the public as to the greater social, cultural and moral good to which they contribute. The decision in England to lift the fee cap so as to enable universities to charge up to £9,000 in annual tuition had the effect of making universities appear more self-interested than they might have liked to appear. Ironically, while the shift of funding from direct government provision to student tuition loans may have provided the only apparent solution to avoiding significant public spending cuts, it undermined to some extent the perception of the university as public good.

Elsewhere in the public sector, debate as to the role expectations of taxpayer-funded services with regard to interaction with citizens is well advanced. The erosion of the size and power of the State as a provider of services has reshaped many agencies and organizations that were previously regarded as unequivocally public. While higher education, particularly in England, is a striking example, evidence of the contestability of public provision can readily be identified in other sectors. In health and social care, several local authorities have contracted out services to private brands such as Virgin Care. Chains of academies and prisons are now run by organizations that are far removed from the direct influence of the civil servant and the taxpayer. Utilities, transportation and mail services are now in private hands, and even government departments are increasingly becoming 'mutualized', so as to operate with at least partial employee ownership.

A definition of public value offered by Leadbeater and Mongon (2008) implies collaborative leadership approaches:

> Public value is developed when public services not only provide services but also create social outcomes that are also valued . . . Public value is created

when educational settings work to improve the wider range of outcomes for their [direct beneficiaries] by engaging with . . . communities in places and processes characterised by equal esteem and equitable authority.

(2008: 22)

Opportunities are now clearly available for universities to lead by example.

CASE STUDY 12: GEORGIA GWINNETT COLLEGE

Georgia Gwinnett is a four-year state college whose mission is to be a twenty-first-century access institution. It was newly-built and launched in 2006 with 118 inaugural students, and has grown rapidly to providing now for almost 10,000. The campus provides beautifully-designed buildings and sports and leisure facilities which are well-used by students. Given the College's mission to engage large numbers of students whose parents did not experience higher education, tuition fees are far from prohibitive. As a result, the current annual cost of attendance for a full-time commuter student is $2,458.

Visiting on a Friday (often a quiet day on US campuses) gives a tangible sense of the engagement and inspiration demonstrated by Georgia Gwinnett's students. It is readily discernible that the College and its organizational culture are built on clear and focused educational principles:

- harnessing innovation in learning technology to support student success;
- providing an integrated educational experience in which service learning and other extra-curricular activities play a key role and are actively managed by the College;
- engagement by all faculty in teaching and mentoring as a hallmark of the institution.

There is a deliberately-stated intention to act as a model for innovation in education and administration. All on-campus services and facilities which are not directly linked to delivering the curriculum are outsourced, and the College was designed in this way from the outset.

The founding President, Dan Kaufman, and current President Stas Preczewski, are both former senior officers from the United States Military Academy at West Point, and they have applied their experience and vision to creating and sustaining an institution which breeds success – the opening sentences of the College prospectus declare unequivocally 'Failure is not an option.'

It is also highly efficient and an institution that understands how to assess its effectiveness. As a start-up institution, the College has needed to recruit enthusiastic teaching faculty staff in significant numbers, with a ratio of applicants per position in the order of around 100 to one. The recruitment process has always signalled clearly that those with aspirations to carry out funded research should look elsewhere for employment.

As one Dean at Georgia Gwinnett put it, people are selected on the basis of 'passion for teaching, and liking students'. Faculty are actively involved in student support, and are expected to be available for students with needs outside class hours. Every course handbook has the cellphone number of the teacher printed clearly on the front cover, and the College-provided phone is meant to elicit a fast response. In addition to providing academic support for students in class and across the campus, Georgia Gwinnett students also access a 24-hour online tutoring service for every major study route offered on campus.

In keeping with the sharp educational focus of the College's pedagogical approaches, the curriculum is geared tightly to the discipline areas which correspond to the greatest employment needs of the catchment area of nearly one million people. Georgia Gwinnett offers only 13 majors, in areas such as Nursing, Special Education, Criminal Justice and Information Technology.

Despite a short history, Georgia Gwinnett has built a strong reputation quickly, and is already ranked in the top ten per cent of colleges nationwide for academic challenge, student/faculty interaction outside of the classroom, and for active and collaborative learning. It has also achieved remarkable results for student retention, performing at least ten percentage points higher than the average for state colleges in their State of Georgia's public system for first-year retention. For a non-selective institution, this pays tribute to the supportive and challenging environment offered to students. It also reflects the practice of having maximum class group sizes of 25, and a compulsory attendance requirement.

The power behind the rapid growth of Georgia Gwinnett's numbers lies in word of mouth: where live-transforming examples of student success affect families, this also impacts on communities, and ultimately, the County and beyond. The most frequently-reported aspect of student feedback is consistently about one aspect: the quality of the teaching staff. The key message which has got around the community is 'Faculty here will help you make it through'.

Leadership

Across the campus, banners reinforce the College's ethos by reiterating four key words which represent its core values: Scholarship, Creativity, Service and Leadership. The last aspect, leadership, is the focus of the rest of the case study.

There is a clear purpose for Georgia Gwinnett, that of inspiring students to contribute to society. This links to the value of service, and is intended to ensure that the College contributes to the long-term civic growth and sustainability of Gwinnett County and its hinterland. Importantly, the current ethnic mix in the County corresponds to the predicted balance for the United States as a whole by 2040. Georgia Gwinnett sees itself as an overt prototype of higher education for the twenty-first century, and is attracting considerable interest from its peers. Not only was it the first new four-year college founded in Georgia in more than 100 years; it was also the first four-year public college created in the United States in the twenty-first century.

Student leadership is developed through setting challenging active learning in class, and through extra-curricular activity, particularly in the student associations and societies funded by College. If a group of students is able to demonstrate that there is demand for establishing a new society, a proposal is made to the College, and if successful, funding is made available. The society's business plan must include concrete outcomes and evaluation measures, which are reviewed after one year. Importantly, those which fail to recruit significant numbers or which do not meet their objectives in the first year are not cut unless they fail to conduct an assessment. If the students running them can produce a reflective, mature analysis which demonstrates learning in practice, they are given even more funding in order to enable them to succeed in the following year. This philosophy of determination to succeed is aligned with the broad educational vision for the institution as a whole.

Leadership is also a key factor in the organization of the College. It was set up deliberately without academic departments or departmental chairs, in order to avoid silo mentalities. Deans therefore manage within a model of distributed leadership, in which clusters of colleagues work together across academic programmes and thematic areas of responsibility overseen by associate deans. Faculty members' offices are deliberately assigned such that no two same-discipline professors may be physically next to one another's office, thus promoting interdisciplinary communication.

In the week when I visited Georgia Gwinnett with a group of leaders from the United Kingdom, the College had just succeeded in securingaccreditation for its degree programmes for a further ten-year period, with feedback from the accrediting body which was extremely positive. One aspect which was found to be an outstanding example of leadership practice concerned strategy: Georgia Gwinnett's strategic plan is a dynamic reality, constantly being updated and enacted. The accrediting body had never before seen this happen so effectively in a higher education institution.

Questions

1 In what ways does an institution you know, or have worked in, take action to review and evaluate how effectively it fulfils its purpose(s)?
2 To what extent do you think it is helpful for a university to consider leadership in its wider implications (rather than simply through formal hierarchical positions), as is the case at Georgia Gwinnett College?

This case study was written by Paul Gentle, following an institutional visit facilitated by Dr Anthony Pinder, Director, Internationalization and Assistant Professor of Education, Georgia Gwinnett College.

7   Systemic action in universities

Cultures of innovation that support agile, strategic working

There are many documented approaches to diagnosing and mapping the extent to which innovation is supported in universities. Bessant et al. (2010) provide a valuable framework for analysing innovation and support in public services, and categorize four dimensions of change. Many institutional leaders report having spent significant time and energy on three of these dimensions; the fourth may be the essential requirement for the future, as we shall see.

Bessant et al.'s dimensions of change (2010: 1–10) are:

- product innovation – changes in product and service offerings
- process innovation – changes in how these offerings are delivered
- position innovation – changes in the context and narrative of engagement with the brand
- paradigm innovation – changes in the underlying mental models of what drives the organization.

In each case, there are simultaneous opportunities for incremental improvements (doing things better) and for radical innovation (doing things differently).

Product innovation is clearly central to the role of university managers, in that the core educational offer as defined by the curriculum, in addition to huge swathes of what is provided by university estates, IT, library, finance, quality and student support services, is constantly subject to recognizable change. Increasingly sophisticated approaches are being used by marketing services to anticipate changing patterns of demand in order to identify trends that feed into a constantly redefined prospectus of what is offered to current and future students.

Process innovation will be similarly familiar to many readers, particularly in light of driving forces towards increased efficiency and modernization (Diamond, 2011). The interest in lean management approaches, developed as a specialism for the higher education context by Cardiff University (Leadership Foundation for Higher Education, 2011), is a classic example of finding ways to remove wasteful elements in existing processes. In terms of the interface with the student experience, the extent to which university procedures have changed to enable online registration, module selection, submitting and receiving feedback on assessment – these are all strong examples of process innovation. The increasing shift towards online provision has led to growth in the proportion of student learning that is mediated online, significantly altering the shape and patterns of usage of physical on-campus facilities such as classrooms and libraries. There has also been growth in outsourcing services that were once thought to be at the core of what universities historically provided themselves.

Position innovation has impacted significantly on practices and mindsets in our universities, too. There are many new channels now open for those seeking to engage with universities. The era of expansion towards mass participation that was seen at its most dramatic in the 1990s in the UK, and considerably earlier in many other nations, was one good example of the opening up of higher education to wider audiences than those considered to be from privileged social classes. Similarly, engagement with employers so as to position particular universities to serve the needs of workforce development could be seen as an example of opening up new markets. The era of mass open online courses (MOOCs) positions universities in a boundary-less, global environment in ways that offer both opportunity and risk to brand images and reputations.

Given the extent of disruption now faced by higher education systems globally (Kennie, 2012), the challenges of paradigm innovation present themselves forcefully. Put starkly, there are decreasing options available to universities that are not prepared to transform the prevailing mental models of what it is they are here to do. The institutions most likely to be under threat to change are those in the 'undifferentiated middle', the institutions that were originally created as publicly funded organizations designed to serve the needs of the State.

The challenge is that the State has moved inexorably to a different deal in which the public appetite for funding universities to do as they themselves wish has diminished in the face of a raft of competing priorities for public spending – including provision of health and welfare services, infrastructure investment and burgeoning retirement pensions. A good example of this shift can be seen in England, where the government minister with responsibility for universities, David Willetts, has used a public rhetoric that insists that universities are no longer public sector organizations. In the case of the significant number of institutions whose direct proportion of income from the State (through the funding council) has decreased from 90% to below 10% between 2011 and 2014, this may well feel to be true. In this period, senior leaders in institutions have described the shift in terms of moving to becoming third sector organizations, operating as not-for-profit charitable bodies. While this is true of their sources of funding, it has not always been reflected in the acknowledgement of the need to reinforce the position of the university as a public and social good.

Paradigm shift, in the case of universities once seen as part of the public sector, is likely to involve a redefinition of relationships between citizens and those who govern and work in our higher education providers (as mentioned in Chapter 6).

Other drivers of paradigm shift are likely to include (Bessant et al., 2010: 12) constant revolution in technology (not only ICT, but increasingly likely to include applications of biotechnology and nanotechnology) and 'the increasingly pressing nature of some 'insoluble' policy problems'. The latter are not defined, but surely must encompass growing inequality, the need for sustainable development, global competition and the decline of the West, and ageing populations. The resultant tensions for the university, which needs to provide a safe space in which high-quality, critical thinking can flourish, and at the same time to defend itself from accusations of behaving as though it is in an ivory tower, are legion. Nevertheless, there appears to be irresistible pressure on universities to reinvent themselves as leaders in reframing and regenerating city regions and their wider hinterlands.

In the absence of major pots of direct funding to incentivize them, there is a danger that taking such a leadership stance may be seen as an expensive option, or possibly even as an unaffordable luxury. This may explain why pro vice-chancellors are sometimes portrayed as jumping on planes to other parts of the globe in pursuit of fee-paying students to fill recruitment gaps, rather than leading change at home. While this represents a caricatured and simplistic view of present realities, it was a commonly reported anecdotal perception in 2013.

Nevertheless, it is not often the case that institutional management structures are primarily driven by acknowledged needs to strengthen innovation, meaning that innovative practices are found towards the edge, rather than at the centre of universities. This can result in the greatest innovators being found on the periphery, often at the interfaces between the institution and its external partners. It may also mean that innovators are marginalized, and feel that their voice is unheard.

It therefore falls to leaders to find ways to champion innovators, nurture the spread of their practices, and include them in the participatory processes of the institution. Maddock (2009) outlines a model that points to three different roles for leaders in public services (Figure 7.1).

Figure 7.1 The role of transforming leaders

In a higher education context, the organizational champions of innovation are to be found on senior management teams, with such titles as Pro Vice-Chancellor or Director of Knowledge Transfer. They are likely to determine and monitor strategy, spearhead key partnership initiatives and design policy supportive of incentivizing innovation.

On the bottom right of the pyramid are the functional and disciplinary heads, responsible for managing departmental units in relatively conservative, stable ways. By virtue of their position in the structure, they are unlikely to challenge the status quo in the organization, and may unwittingly or sometimes intentionally exclude those who are more capable of innovation. The innovators thus occupy the periphery, and may focus their energies beyond the organization rather than internally.

The third category of leader in Maddock's model, in the centre of the pyramid, plays a significant role in spanning boundaries in order to make change happen, and in particular to harness innovation in the interests of the organization. These are typically those directors of knowledge transfer or associate deans who are skilled at facilitating learning conversations, and whose networked knowledge of a wide range of players (both within and outwith political hierarchies) puts them in a strong position as transformation catalysts. Such leaders are classic examples of what Hawkins and Winter (1997) call the 'lifeblood of the learning organisation'.

In organizations in which rigid structures prevail, Maddock's model may hold good for some time to come. However, there are institutions that have moved towards creating a cultural architecture that incorporates a high degree of agility. At the same time as universities have moved palpably towards becoming 'businesslike', many knowledge-intensive companies have deliberately sought to be 'university-like'. These organizations locate themselves on what they design as campuses, both physical and virtual, and expect their workforces to behave like faculty. They enjoy considerable professional autonomy and other aspects of the 'psychological contract' that prevail in universities.

Doz and Kosonen (2008) identify the characteristics of strategic agility, categorizing these in three groupings, the first of which they describe as *sharpening strategic sensitivity*. This involves processes that enable strategy to be formed openly, in a participative manner, rather than by a senior team working in isolation from the rest of the organization. Views and insights from outside the organization are brought in systemically – partly by encouraging people to get out and discover worlds beyond the company and the segment it occupies, and also by engaging in dialogue with stakeholders in which fresh perspectives are shared. Further measures that support sharper strategic thinking and working include active encouragement of personal experimentation by individuals, and developing capability in identifying and remaining open to future trends.

As mentioned in the previous chapter, the Leadership Foundation for Higher Education attempts to nurture such practices by designing experiences in which groups of higher education leaders engage with strategic challenges that are set for them by senior leaders in organizations that are not universities. Using a process of inquiry, they carry out a piece of group consultancy, using documentary evidence, interviews with employees, and focus groups, before presenting a set of recommendations to the host organization. As well as providing fascinating insights into other working cultures, the experiences provide rich data as a basis for feedback and reflective learning for participants. In the heat of real-time action in an authentic and usually complex task, the university leaders make mistakes, and facilitators enable them to learn from these. They also note many positive examples of the impact of their behaviours and language on others, and use these as a basis for modifying their practices in their own institutional settings.

We have also facilitated a number of events within universities in which strategy has been developed using open processes of participation. When used successfully, such events can enable large numbers of people to generate ideas or comment on proposals in ways that help to shape key decisions.

RESOURCE 23: USING COLLABORATIVE ACTIVITIES CUMULATIVELY

Here is an example of how a combination of the resources described in earlier chapters was used to create a sequence of activity during a morning that brought together institutional governors, academic staff, students and senior managers.

We introduced a sequence of activities that asked participants to work through four student-focused core themes of:

- recruitment
- satisfaction
- attainment
- employability.

People were seated around circular tables in mixed groups of 10 or 11 (governors, managers and Academic Board members, including the Student Union president). Each table group then rotated in turn around the themed tables, working according to a different set of instructions at each stage.

1   Evaluation of current practice at the institution for the theme in question. Using a flipchart at each table, individuals in table groups spend five minutes writing Post-Its in response to three different categories, and paste them on the chart: *What's working well?/What's so-so?/What's not working well?* Groups then discuss what actions could be taken in response to the ideas on the flipchart, creating new Post-Its for how to: Celebrate or communicate success (*What's working well?*); Quick Wins (*What's so-so?*); Key Challenges (*What's not working well?*).
2   After the first rotation, new groups spend 15 minutes refining or adding to what the previous group has left on its evaluation chart.

3   On arriving at their third theme, people use Post-its to think through how they would like two respective groupings of key stakeholders (Students and Academic Staff) to respond once the strategy is fully in place: 'By July 2013, what do we want [Students or Academic Staff] to Say . . ./Feel . . ./See . . ./Do . . .?'

4   At the final themed table, people consider the stakeholder visions created by the previous group, and decide what changes are needed in staff behaviours and organizational culture in the institution.

Having completed all four stages in a sequence lasting around 75 minutes, groups return to their original starting point, and consider how to summarize the key messages coming from the work that has been done on their theme. These key messages are then presented back in plenary.

These activities clearly generate considerable energy and engagement from participants, and provide rich data for institutions to gather and feed into strategic planning processes. While one governor described the outcome in terms of his own feelings of 'information overload', most participants appreciated the opportunity to be involved actively, and to have a voice using an approach that was very different from a board or committee meeting.

Academic staff could readily see opportunities for transferring some of the activities to their own pedagogical practices, and some colleagues were evidently motivated by the vision of the student experience that had built up during the course of a morning's work.

Doz and Kosonen's second grouping of characteristics focuses on *resource fluidity*. This conjures up an image that is opposite to that of rigid silo working, in which departments do not communicate laterally, and where internal competition fans the flames around which robber barons dance with glee. Fluidity enables all kinds of resources – money, people, equipment, information, access to power – to flow to parts of an organization where they are needed in order to support strategy. This de-emphasizes structure, and highlights processes and systems. One practical example that is often seen in agile organizations is that of rotating management roles and of teams that are formed rapidly (and then disbanded equally rapidly when their strategic goals are fulfilled).

While project teams are common in universities, the idea of rotating responsibilities is less developed. Perhaps the closest higher education institutions come to this can be found in the practice of fixed-term academic management positions, in roles such as Head of Department, Dean and Pro Vice-Chancellor. Here, there is (at least in the UK) a distinction between different categories of university. Those that see themselves as more research-intensive are more likely to use rotating management roles. However, the idea of rotation is only rarely seen as a means to enhancing management capability. It is often conceived of as a way of confining the damage that might be caused to a research career to a relatively limited period of time. Bolden et al. postulate that:

> the managerial and performance management concerns of heads of departments are now so overwhelming that there is simply no time to engage in intellectual leadership; in fact anyone who wants to maintain prominence in an intellectual field may feel it is best to avoid such jobs.
>
> (2012: 35)

Nevertheless, at the end of their brief period of tenure in such a role (typically three or four years), some individuals can find themselves caught in a dilemma over whether or not to continue to pursue an emerging interest in management, and particularly in the aspects of the role pertaining to leadership.

The third characteristic of strategic agility, and the one of most direct relevance to the subject of this book, is that of *building collective commitment*. Doz and Kosonen cite key enablers as high-quality internal dialogue, conflict and energized action, and time for reflection. Let us consider each of these in turn, in the context of practices – and potential practices – in universities.

High-quality internal dialogue

This is typified by the kinds of activity outlined in Chapter 3, under the headings of learning conversations and action learning, as well as the approaches to meetings described in Chapter 4. Doz and Kosonen also underline the importance of diversity: 'People of different sensitivities, areas of expertise, cultural origins, age, gender, and types of intelligence need to be brought together in a structured, purposeful dialogue' (2008: 23). This is quite different from the 'groupthink' that might result from a closed and exclusive grouping of people talking intensely within a familiar configuration, such as a senior management team.

Doz and Kosonen highlight what is different about the process they have in mind:

> This dialogue, as opposed to debate, means a conversation where participants share assumptions and explain the logic of their thought, rather than affirm conclusions and present arguments . . . Expressing difference or dissent in a corporate hierarchy is often difficult, and potentially costly, yet it is essential to strategic sensitivity.
>
> (2008: 23)

They point out the difficulties inherent in finding time for dialogue when in practice resources are heavily committed to operational activity. It becomes difficult to hold conversations about complex strategic issues, and even if these are attempted, it is difficult for them to be objective: seeing and discussing the university from a distance is difficult if one is immersed in the internal language and accompanying emotional charge that have been built up within the institution.

One measure suggested by Doz and Kosonen is the use of skilled internal consultants who can combine broad knowledge of the organization with conceptually challenging approaches. They are likely to bring soundly tested frameworks for conversations that 'allow rich interpretations of strategic questions' (2008: 73). For universities, this will certainly involve a conscious process of capacity building, but may not necessarily mean expensive hiring-in of skills. It may be feasible to harness the expertise that the institution is already selling to other organizations through academic knowledge transfer activities, and to channel this skill set to serve the case of improved strategic decision-making internally.

Other measures include deliberately selecting top team members for diversity, creating shadow management teams (for instance, inviting young high-potential middle leaders to devise an organizational long-term vision), and extending strategy dialogue across the organization. This last measure is arguably the only one that is relatively common in higher education; widespread consultation exercises and management away days will be familiar to many readers, who will also be aware of the possibilities and constraints associated with these activities.

Conflict

There is much evidence in the literature, and in the experiences that individual leaders bring with them to developmental programmes, to support the notion that people working in organizations find it challenging to deal with conflict. Furthermore, they often prefer to avoid handling the challenges that arise, circumnavigating the many 'difficult' men and women who appear to surround them. Where they do not shy away from conflict, they apply a range of tactics to resolve differences through negotiating, accommodating, competing or collaborating (Thomas and Kilmann, 1974). Collaborating results where there is both a high degree of equality of assertiveness from all parties involved and a strong disposition towards co-operating. In such situations, working relationships are likely to improve and integrated solutions are likely to be found for the organization. At the same time, learning is manifest, and often celebrated, and the outcome can be one of strengthened commitment to the organization and its goals. Since collaborating requires and develops skills involving the application of empathy, listening and understanding, it favours those with high emotional intelligence. This approach to potential conflict does not hide from or avoid dissent – rather, it ensures that such dissent becomes constructive.

Grint (2005) identifies four categories of consent or dissent, which vary according to the extent to which a working culture is one of dependence on a leader figure, and to the degree of commitment to community (rather than individual) goals.

High dependence and strong individual commitment result in destructive consent, in which people appear to agree (for instance, in meetings that reluctantly vote through decisions originating from a hierarchical leader), but then undermine group decisions by failing to enact them.

High dependence in a context of collective commitment is likely to lead to constructive consent, in which organizational behaviours can seem enticingly harmonious, but can often lead to 'groupthink' that lacks criticality and is potentially blind to the extent to which a reified leader fails to develop autonomous capabilities in followers, who in turn behave as disciples. The absence of the leader, for whatever reason, is likely to bring about an inability to make decisions or take action.

Highly independent and individualistic working cultures – arguably those often prevailing in stereotypical academic departments – lead to the characterization of the leader as 'cat herder', and to a climate of anarchy in which destructive dissent is the dominant discourse. Many readers will be able to think of cultures with these characteristics that they have encountered, if not actually worked in.

The culture that is likely to appeal most to those with a collective orientation and a preference for empowering colleagues is also that in which constructive dissent thrives. Grint calls this a heterarchical culture, in which leaders emerge where called for by situational demands, rather than because of their formal positions or grading. Members of the community act responsibly, demonstrating what might be interpreted as combined maturity in both leadership and followership. Individuals are capable of switching between the two as demanded by given situations. The image Grint uses for the leader in this culture is that of the wheelwright, whose crafted outcome is an artefact in which strength and efficacy depend on the combined total of the capacity of each individual spoke.

Energized action

Arguing that 'the main target of an adaptive leader is to make other people "shine" and excel in the company by reducing obstacles and fear in the organization', Doz and Kosonen stress that the 'energy and joy stemming from finding a solution and from being forgiven after a failed attempt to try something new cannot be underestimated' (2008: 89). They reflect on the dangers of failing to attend to the emotional health of the organization, including those of scepticism over senior leaders' skills and capabilities. At the same time, they emphasize the challenge of bringing energy, drive and commitment to a mature organization.

They outline actions that leaders can take to draw on the power of emotions in developing strategic agility (2008: 172–4). The first of these involves supporting people in doing the kind of work in which they experience the greatest possible sense of pride and self-efficacy. Leading towards an emotional state where people in an organization feel valuable and valued can yield strong results.

The second action taps into shared emotional contexts. If leaders can find moments in the previous history of the organization that resonate with their workforce, these are likely to be potential sources of energy. Examples would include recalling when and how the department achieved its greatest recent success, or what it felt like when people overcame adversity together. The concept of emotional signatures (Shaw, 2007) may be helpful. Shaw outlines a range of different emotional states that define the correlations between (in the context of higher education) how staff and students feel about the institution and the extent to which particular emotional states can add value to the reputation and identity of the organization. The most positive emotional states, where individuals feel valued, cared for, trusted and safe, are likely to lead to what Shaw defines as 'recommending' actions. The most desirable state of all leads to actions of 'advocacy' for the institution, and is likely to be engendered by the individual feeling delighted by expectations that have been exceeded, and feeling empowered.

Thirdly, creating and sustaining a culture of care builds a sense of trust and confidence in people, and motivates them to want to support each other. Doz and Kosonen underline the importance of emotions being neither repressed nor criticized. This applies to top teams as well as to the qualities of leadership demonstrated throughout the organization.

The fourth action concerns reinforcing the purpose of the organization (*pace* Collini, 2012), and using this to generate a higher meaning for people in terms of how they see their work.

Time for reflection

Spending time thinking about doing, or having done, something – rather than actually doing it – seems counterintuitive. There always appears to be something more pressing to attend to, especially in a world that requires swift action in order to deal with immediate crises. Advocates of slow thinking, however, argue that such behaviour represents a false economy, and is unsustainable.

Investment in deliberative processes that support high-quality thinking, such as those advocated by Nancy Kline (1999), can result in more stable and supportive working environments in which those who work in them are likely to be considerably more engaged and productive.

Those who set aside time for creative or strategic thinking are likely to find this rewarded by a better sense of balance between short-term detail and 'big picture' thinking. Being able to switch consciously between one and the other, rather than being trapped on what feels like a treadmill of daily routine, may be more than a luxury – it may be an essential capability of working in the university of the future.

In addition to calling for good time-management skills, making time and space to envision and build scenarios is likely to draw on some lessons from Neuro-Linguistic Programming (NLP). NLP proponents such as Agness offer a range of techniques for obtaining the necessary sense of flow, including moving one's locus of energy, or chakra, from within to outside and beyond the body (2013: 127–131).

There is a growing trend towards appointing senior leaders into universities from other sectors, and this brings with it a wide range of challenges to how higher education institutions work. The drivers – and associated discourses – for making such appointments (not only to Vice-Chancellor positions, but also to roles such as Chief Operating Officer, Dean of Faculty or Director of Professional Services) are multiple. They include the perceived needs for increased efficiency, modernization, commercialization, collaboration and for providing institutions with a stronger political voice. Often a set of views is expressed about the extent to which academics should change their working practices and cultures. Likewise, adjustments of mindset are sometimes called for on the part of those entering management roles from outside the higher education sector; some do not survive the transition process involved.

Among the common sector backgrounds from which such managers are drawn successfully, fairly significant numbers are drawn from the public health sector. These bring with them their own ways of seeing the world, and new sets of practices that inform processes of innovation.

One interesting comparison lies in the ways in which the UK's National Health Service (NHS) has engaged patients in shaping the experiences they have in their contacts and relationships with it. It is interesting to consider how the concept of the 'expert patient' translates into universities. Is there such a thing as an 'expert student'? Some leaders, particularly senior university managers with prior experience of leadership in health professions, have begun to experiment with this concept. In some cases, they have drawn on the processes evolved by the NHS around the concept of Experience-Based Design.

However, such transfer across sectors meets only with qualified success, and the health sector is frequently critiqued for the approaches it brings to innovation and change. Mowles et al. (2010) point to the dangers of conceiving organizations as systems, or attempting to manage them as biological organisms. Instead, he stresses the relevance of applying scientific complexity theory in order to understand how innovation and change actually occur. In particular, managers' intentions for action are rarely achieved because these intentions are in constant interplay with the other intentions of those whom they seek to engage, and are unlikely to be fully aligned. As a result, negotiations need to take place that are set in the context of relationships (which require skilful understanding and handling of a vast range of micropolitics), and the outcomes are rarely predictable.

Stacey (2013) recounts a conversation that occurred during a consultancy project in which he was working with two very senior police officers (the Chief Constable and Deputy Chief Constable from a County force). As consultant, Stacey asked the officers if they felt in control of their organization. 'Of course not!' flashed the reply, followed hastily by the confession, 'but we can't tell anybody that!'

Mowles et al. claim that the lack of predictability of being able to realize one's intentions does not mean that 'there is no point in managers forming plans and acting according to their best judgements' (2010: 123). Nevertheless, they advise against assuming that change occurs through programmes and initiatives, where those affected often report fatigue: 'change in innovation often arises despite or in opposition to change programmes' (2010: 123).

Greater attention should be paid, according to Mowles et al., to the distinction between what they call 'public transcripts' and 'hidden transcripts' – what is broadcast to wide audiences as opposed to the private conversations that reveal people's personal and political interpretations of what occurs.

They advocate that managers 'spend more time discussing and reflecting upon how they are caught up in the particular game they are currently obliged to play with others' (2010: 123).

One approach to narrowing the gaps between the public and hidden transcripts might be to bring into the open discussions around the extent to which universities operate within the cultures of deference that we discussed in Chapter 4.

Sustainable practices
Ensuring that leaders and institutions don't burn out

Fullan and Scott argue for 'turnaround leadership' in which they call for fundamental changes in the priorities and behaviours of leaders in universities. In making a sustained argument for effective leadership for turbulent times, they underline the importance of:

- a greater capacity for enacting change, through rapid prototyping of potentially viable solutions to problems rather than debating them *ad nauseam* through committees (which they describe as a 'Ready, Fire, Aim Approach') (Fullan and Scott, 2009: 85)
- recognizing the need for 'a critical mass of key leaders – centrally and locally – to intentionally model in their daily behaviours the attributes and capabilities they want the university to develop' (2009: 102)
- ensuring the sustainability of the institution by paying attention to the extent to which administrative processes add value (2009: 109)
- selecting and rewarding staff based on their emotional intelligence, alongside their intellectual capacities (2009: 133).

Gitsham (2012) reports on the outcomes of facilitating a number of collaborative conversations with business leaders around the topic of the importance of the contribution made by senior private sector executives to huge contemporary societal issues.

These conversations highlighted a growing connection being made by leaders between understanding the forces that shape society and creating value for their businesses. Evidence was generated of a new leadership function of leading change beyond business boundaries, through:

- contributing to public debate with an informed point of view
- proactively leading change in consumer and supplier behaviour, industry norms and government policy
- relating well with multiple constituencies
- engaging in dialogue to understand and empathize with groups and communities with perspectives contrary to one's own
- engaging in multi-stakeholder collaboration with unconventional partners.

These examples will be familiar to many senior managers in higher education, though it might be argued that such an externally oriented focus remains a rarity, given the energy being expended on constant, inward-looking change (such as restructuring, business reprocessing, curriculum overhaul).

The challenge being acknowledged by business leaders provokes much thought in relation to the behaviours of senior managers in higher education, who have arguably not championed the public good represented by universities as actively as they might have (perhaps assuming that it is self-evident):

> In trying to come to terms with how to satisfy shifting market demand for an improved quality of life in an increasingly resource-constrained context, business leaders have been forced to chart a new path and rethink and redefine how they create long term value, adopting measures of success that go beyond just short-term shareholder value to embrace a much broader range of indicators of 'stakeholder value'.
>
> (Gitsham, 2012: 8–9)

This places the concept of sustainability at the heart of the matter. The practices of adaptive leadership (Heifetz et al., 2009) are called for in large measure, and this raises some interesting questions about the implications for the work of leaders in higher education.

The first concerns how we might challenge manifestations of what can appear to be an attractive set of strengths in hard times; those of the heroic leader, characterized by Gitsham as 'aggressiveness, strength, drive, ambition and self-reliance' (2012: 17). The alternative (and perhaps the only sustainable approach), is to 'value leadership that is collective and cooperative and focuses on asking the right questions rather than having all the answers' (2012: 17).

This means exercising qualities of moral courage, of daring to raise difficult questions in the interests of addressing both opportunities and dangers for the organization – at all levels in the hierarchy. Instead of directing people autocratically, leadership requires setting challenges, then supporting underlying processes that enable people to succeed in meeting the challenges. These processes include cross-fertilization of knowledge across and between diverse organizational units.

In order to embed necessary shifts in organizational culture, it is important to devise metrics against which to gauge successful improvement. Such metrics are likely to begin with establishing a baseline by seeking the subjective views of organizational members as to what drives its behaviours and practices.

Diagnosing the culture using an instrument such as the Collaborative Working Survey not only is one way of eliciting views, but it also provides opportunities for conversations, which might be shaped around questions such as the examples given after the survey itself.

RESOURCE 24: COLLABORATIVE WORKING SURVEY

This survey is a diagnostic tool to take the pulse of the collaborative effort in a working team.

This will diagnose areas that are going well as well as identifying areas where tensions exist. Tensions should be explored through dialogue and reflective practice to clarify the nature of difficulties and plan how to go forward.

The survey can be repeated over time to assess development and progress as the collaboration evolves.

Table 7.1 Collaborative working survey

We have developed common aims.	1	2	3	4
We have developed shared compatible aims.	1	2	3	4
There is good communication between members.	1	2	3	4
There is clarity about each member's role and who/what they represent.	1	2	3	4
There are deepening bonds of commitment and determination between members to achieve the aims.	1	2	3	4
Members are prepared to compromise in the interests of the common aims.	1	2	3	4
We have developed effective working processes, which helps get things done.	1	2	3	4
There is accountability between members for following through on decisions that have been agreed.	1	2	3	4
The leadership of the collaboration enacts principles of democracy and equality to empower everyone to take an active role.	1	2	3	4
Members share resources.	1	2	3	4
Members do not undermine each other or behave in ways that have a negative impact on others.	1	2	3	4
Members trust each other to behave in ways that show respect.	1	2	3	4
Power (personal and role) is used wisely to avoid over-control by any one member.	1	2	3	4
Due to working together we make faster, better decisions.	1	2	3	4
Members share information and knowledge.	1	2	3	4
Members are recognized and appreciated for their contribution.	1	2	3	4
There is productive output as a result of our collaboration.	1	2	3	4
The synergy achieved through collaboration makes things happen that wouldn't or couldn't otherwise.	1	2	3	4
Individual total				

Steps

1   Distribute the survey to all members of the collaborative effort.
2   Ask each member individually to rate the extent to which they think the themes are present in the current collaborative working arrangements.
3   Collate the scores.
4   Present the collated scores to the group, highlighting areas that are strong, areas where there is a diverse range of views and areas where tensions seem to exist.

In following up responses from team members to the survey, the following questions might make for a productive conversation.

Questions to ask about the results

• What seem to be your strengths? (High percentages of colleagues agreeing that topics are both important and currently happening.)
• What might you conclude if there is a high percentage of 'disagree' ratings?
• What does it mean when people regard an issue as important but feel it isn't currently happening? Follow-up questions include: *Why isn't it happening?* and *What may need to be done about this?*
• What does it mean when colleagues don't consider an issue very important?
• What will you now do with the results? (Adapted from NCSL, 2006)

RESOURCE 25: ORGANIZATIONAL DIAGNOSTICS

Another approach to seeking views is that proposed by the team responsible for the project 'Taking the Pulse of your Institution'. Here, a narrow range of questions is put anonymously to a given population of organizational members in order to build a composite picture. The project team suggests that greater trust is sometimes placed by respondents if a third party organization (rather than the HR department within the respondents' own institution, for instance) receives and collates the responses.

The questions used are generative, in that they can be applied to a wide range of settings and context, and can also form the basis of productive learning conversations. If these conversations are seen to result in action being taken to improve organizational climate, this is likely to result in a greater degree of trust in the organization, and of willingness to contribute to innovation processes.

Tables 7.2 and 7.3 give two sets of examples used in practice. The first concerns the extent to which individuals working in a department feel supported by the organizational culture. The second seeks feedback on perceptions of practices concerning equality and diversity. Finally, in order to be truly effective at playing the part of good citizen, leaders in universities should consider how they might redouble their efforts to influence policymakers, at local, national and international levels. Higher education institutions are full of researchers whose impact is measured significantly by the influence they have amongst peers in their discipline. The fact that this cannot yet be said to be fully true for university leaders indicates something of the magnitude of the journey ahead.

Table 7.2 Support from the organizational culture (adapted from HEFCE, 2010b)

	Yes, strongly	*Yes*	*Not really*	*No*	*Not applicable*
1 Good communication is a characteristic of this department.					
2 This department's staff and senior managers support each other.					
3 There are good working relationships between staff.					
4 My administrative load is about right.					
5 I am able to have a good work/life balance.					
6 Well-focused staff development is available to me.					
7 I have most of the resources I need to support my work.					
8 The department's accommodation functions well in support of my work.					
9 (Department-specific bespoke question)					
10 (Department-specific bespoke question)					

Table 7.3 Perceptions of equality and diversity (adapted from HEFCE, 2010b)

	Yes, strongly	*Yes*	*Not really*	*No*	*Not applicable*
1 I am sure managers here are familiar with discrimination legislation.					
2 I am confident my manager would act upon a complaint concerning discrimination.					
3 It is my experience that this campus is free from discrimination against staff from minority backgrounds.					
4 In my opinion career progression works in practice for staff of all backgrounds.					
5 I feel sure that intimidation of staff from minority backgrounds does not take place here.					
6 I believe that equal opportunity for staff of all backgrounds is a reality here.					

CASE STUDY 13: UNIVERSITY OF BEDFORDSHIRE
Carbon management

Background

A growing body of research continues to show the importance of addressing and tackling climate change. It is vital that the university sector as a whole reduces its carbon footprint, and becomes more sustainable. This provides important messages not just for the universities themselves, but for the wider communities of which they are a part.

The University of Bedfordshire took the initiative to set up an Environment Action Team, who produced a detailed picture of the university's carbon footprint, and evaluated suggested means of reducing it. This research has led to a culture in the organization whereby reduction of the institution's carbon footprint is now embedded.

The problem, monitoring mechanisms and results envisaged

Cutting CO_2 emissions as part of the fight against climate change should be a key priority for universities, thereby getting 'our own house in order' and leading by example. The Higher Education Carbon Management programme (Carbon Trust, 2006) has been designed to assist universities like the University of Bedfordshire in saving money on energy and putting it to good use in other areas, while making a positive contribution to the environment by lowering their CO_2 emissions.

The university conducted a 10-month project to establish its carbon footprint and to look for cost-effective ways of reducing it. The report calculated carbon emissions associated with the university's direct activities, including energy use, travel, and water, and considered the implications of indirect activities including deliveries and waste.

Electricity was by far the single largest source. All the university's electricity is taken from the grid, so is mostly derived from fossil fuels. Space and water heating is also a substantial contributor, with travel, chiefly staff commuting, following (see Table 7.4).

Table 7.4 Carbon dioxide emissions by source, 2006/07

Source	Tonnes CO_2	% of total
Staff commuting	867.0	10.5%
Staff business travel	124.6	1.5%
Fleet, including shuttle buses	97.1	1.2%
Electricity	4,497.9	54.3%
Fossil fuels	2,661.6	32.2%
Water	28.6	0.3%
Total	8,276.8	100%

Without any effort to curb energy use, and assuming prices continue to rise, this means the university is likely to see its energy bills rise from £1.2 million in 2006/07 to £1.7 million by 2014/15. However, with action taken to cut energy use by 5% in the first year, and 3% per year thereafter, utilities spend should remain constant despite price rises, and the university's carbon footprint would drop from 8430 tonnes of carbon dioxide per annum to 6470 tonnes.

However, further action will need to be taken if the university is to meet its targets, and further to contribute towards the government's proposed target of an 80% cut in carbon dioxide emissions by 2050. This is not, therefore, a single project, but should be regarded as the first step in a long campaign.

Environment policy

The following policy statement was adopted by the university and approved by the Corporate Management Team. It became university policy in May 2007.

The University of Bedfordshire recognizes that all of the activities it undertakes have some impact on the local environment as well as worldwide. The university is fully committed to minimising this impact as much as possible and seeks the support of all staff, students, visitors, contractors and suppliers to contribute to achieving this goal.

The university is committed to developing an ongoing programme to:

- develop policy and strategies in a co-ordinated manner, taking full account of any environmental implications;
- place environmental factors at the forefront of any significant decisions on the university's existing operations and future plans;
- promote and encourage the use of sustainable forms of transport by staff and students;
- promote effective waste management and recycling practices;
- minimize harmful emissions released into the atmosphere and help to conserve valuable resources for future generations through improvements to energy efficiency;
- increase the awareness of environmental responsibilities among staff, students and visitors to the university through guidelines and training;
- meet the requirements of relevant legislation and strive for continuous improvement in environmental performance.

The policy will be reviewed annually.

Opportunities for carbon savings

The work of the carbon management team, and the surveys conducted by the Carbon Trust, have identified a number of opportunities for making energy savings. Those that have been costed, and have likely payback periods of below two years, are listed in Tables 7.5 and 7.6.

Prioritized actions, costs and savings

Table 7.6 shows the projects that were prioritized in 2010, their associated costs and the savings envisaged. The Strategic Implementation Plan was compiled with the help of many key staff and the Director, Facilities and Estates. The plan should not be seen as a one-off document, but rather as the first stage in a long-term project. The university has an important role to play, both in adjusting its own practices to a low-carbon future and in

Table 7.5 Project costs and savings

Category	Project	CO_2 savings, tonnes/year	Estimated cost (£)	Payback period, years
University-wide	Energy Monitoring & Management	12	17,500	0.6
Structural projects, Luton	Boiler Inhibiter Controls	40	2,500	0.4
	Re-lamping	53	8,000	0.8
	Heating zones	30	7,500	1.8
	Voltage power optimizer	90	35,000	1.9
	Lighting controls	100	40,000	1.95
Structural projects, Bedford	Lighting controls	50	18,000	1.8
	Re-lamping	50	10,000	1
Structural projects, Putteridge Bury	Replace boiler	200	70,000 from planned maintenance	N/A
IT projects	Computer shut-down	64	None	Immediate
Waste management	Extended recycling	N/A	N/A	N/A
Behavioural change	Communications Plan	4	2,000	0.2
Total		693	210,000 (including Putteridge Bury boiler)	

Table 7.6 Priorities, costs and savings

Project	Cost (£)	Annual savings (£)	Annual savings (tonnes CO_2)	Payback time (years)
Communications Plan	2,000	10,000	40	0.2
Energy Monitoring & Management	17,500	30,000	350	0.6
Automatic Computer Switch-off	2,000	12,000	64	0.2
Putteridge Bury Boiler	70,000 (planned maintenance)		50–200	
Lighting Occupancy Controls	60,000	30,000	150	2
Re-lamping	10,000	5,000	53	2

embedding a low-carbon culture in the wider community. Although this will take time, it presents a huge opportunity for the university to recover the high ground and once more establish a reputation for being one of the most environmentally considerate universities in the region.

Questions

1   Are there aspects of carbon management that on the face of this case study the university is missing?
2   How is your university taking forward carbon management?
3   How is this being communicated, and how are staff taking ownership of this development?

Case study developed by Professor M.J.C. Crabbe, Executive Dean, University of Bedfordshire, and Professor Dawn Forman.

CASE STUDY 14: UNIVERSIDAD DE LA SABANA
Sustainable growth

Overview

The Department for Business, Innovation and Skills has indicated its view on what is needed for sustainable growth and leadership in further and higher education (DBIS 2010a, 2010b, 2011). Encouragement through these reports has been not only to educate students, irrespective of whether this education is in further education, publicly funded universities or privately funded universities, but to provide them with academic skills and also the technical skills needed by employers.

This encouragement is to enable further and higher education institutions to play their part not only in securing sustainable growth in education at this level but also in facilitating economic growth in the country.

This case study invites us to consider how the Universidad de La Sabana, Bogotá, Colombia has been developed with such aspirations in mind.

Background: Colombia and Bogotá

Over the past 65 years substantial improvements have been made in Latin America with regard to life expectancy (Crisp, 2010). Between 1950 and 2005 life expectancy increased by:

- 27 years in Asia, to 68
- 23 years in Latin America and the Caribbean, to 73

- 23 years in the Middle East, to 67
- 14 years in Oceania, to 74
- 11 years in Sub-Saharan Africa, to 49
- 9 years in North America, to 78
- 8 years in Europe, to 74.

Life expectancy in low- and middle-income countries increased more than in high-income countries between 1950 and 2005 (United Nations, 2007).

Colombia is the third largest economy in South America (Wikipedia 2013a). However, in 2009, 46% of the population lived below the poverty line and 17% in extreme poverty. As usual, poverty, health and educational achievement mirror economic factors: Colombia's economic profile is shown in Figure 7.2.

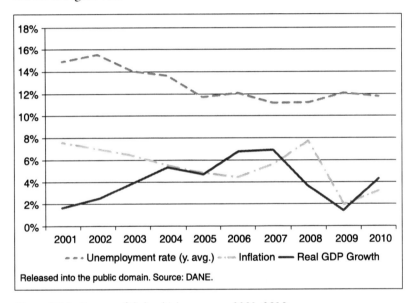

Figure 7.2 Indicators of Colombia's economy 2001–2010

Public spending on higher education in Colombia as a proportion of Gross Domestic Product was 4.7%, one of the highest in Latin America. Funding for education is enhanced by private funding and, as a deeply Roman Catholic country, much of this private funding comes from Opus Dei.

Bogotá has a population of 8,840,116 and, as Colombia is said to be in the middle of the Americas, Bogotá is in the middle of Colombia – halfway between the blue waters of the Caribbean and the highest white peaks of the Andes.

The Universidad de La Sabana

The Universidad de La Sabana is a private higher education institution founded in 1979 (Wikipedia, 2013b) and is therefore one of Colombia's youngest universities. Despite its youth the university was awarded the Highest Quality Institutional Accreditation by the National Ministry of Education in 2006 and was one of only 16 Colombian universities to receive this award. In 2011 it was ranked 170th in the Latin American university ranking of 3,491 universities and 2,348 in the world ranking of 19,403 (Ranking Web of World Universities, 2011).

Sustainability

The Universidad de La Sabana has achieved international standing in a short period of time and, while its student numbers are relatively small at 8,500, the university runs 18 undergraduate programmes, 31 specialization programmes and five Master's programmes. The university also has 21 research groups that are classified by Colciencias, the government office that certifies the quality of research groups in Colombia (Wikipedia, 2013b). While it is a private institution, it is very clear about its commitment to sustainable growth of the local economy and to providing opportunities to lower socio-economic groups. In Colombia six levels of social banding are recognized, and the university ensures that 40% of its students come from the lowest 2 levels of the social grouping. Half of these students will receive a fee reduction or waiver. The university believes that by educating these groups, not only the individuals but their families and the community as a whole will benefit.

The university believes that its achievements to date are due to:

- prioritizing –
  o intellectual capital
  o international mobility
  o scientific progress
  o strong social accountability strategies despite being a private organization

- providing –
  o clear leadership
  o innovation
  o research
  o internationalization

- Key also to its achievements are its values, which embrace –
  o viewing people as individuals
  o encouraging an interdisciplinary approach

o   contributing to society through high-quality provision in a friendly environment that is focused on the family
o   offering voluntary tutoring assistance in career development by professors.

These factors collectively, the institution believes, will enable it not only to maintain its position but to provide sustainable growth for the future.

Recovery after a disaster

While the university has demonstrated the foundations for growth and sustainability, the real test of sustainability comes when unforeseen disaster strikes.

At 9.30 on 25 April 2011, owing to a break of the containment jetty, the Bogotá River flooded 90% of the university; classes were cancelled, the electricity supply was interrupted, substantial material losses were experienced and the university was said to be completely dislodged (Latin America Current Events and News, 2011). Flooding actually occurred twice to the university, but such is the commitment of the community of Bogotá to the university making a difference to the skills and economic needs of the country that offers were made to house classes while the university recovered. Staff of the university therefore provided classes in a variety of settings, modifying their provision accordingly, and none of the classes were cancelled.

While the costs of re-establishing the institution ran to over a million dollars, the university also invested in building barriers to the river wall and ensuring water could be diverted in the event of future climatic changes. Three months after the initial floods the university was back and fully running within its refurbished buildings.

Questions

1   How does your institution contribute to the skills and economic needs of its country or region?
2   What factors are important for sustainable growth of an institution?
3   Following unpredicted setbacks, what will facilitate quick recovery to a sustainable future?

Based on work from Forman, D., Jones, M. and Thistlethwaite, J. (eds) (2014) *Leadership Development for Interprofessional Education and Collaborative Practice.* (Palgrave Macmillan, with licence to use provided by Palgrave MacMillan).

Ways forward for the sector
*Towards a learning-rich, relationship-intense,
leadership culture*

For all that learning is central to the role of educational institutions, it nevertheless continues to appear to take us by surprise when universities fail to apply the lessons that result from their mistakes. Knee-jerk reactions prevail, short-term solutions are imposed, and managers reshuffled, all too often on grounds of personality politics.

By the end of a decade that has so far seen enormous surges forward in the extent to which universities engage seriously in the challenges offered by the internet, it seems certain that job roles will have changed fundamentally compared with the situation in 2010. Increasing differentiation between funded researchers and 'teaching and scholarship' staff will probably have led to a wide spectrum of job types among groupings of people who were collectively known as academics.

As emergent business models become more viable around the development of MOOCs, it seems likely that increasing numbers of university staff will be providing mentoring to students who learn in an enriched environment in which interactive understanding and application of knowledge are mediated largely online (as in the example of the collaborative partnership in California, San Jose *State University Udacity Plus*, pioneered in 2013). Such developments would seem to play into the hands of advocates of collaborative, learning-focused leadership.

Gauntlett et al. raise fascinating issues concerning the changing shape of human experience due to the possibilities of multimedia and internet-based collaborative tools (2012: 93). Since human brains and bodies are changing physiologically as they adapt to the learning and transformation that results from increasingly interactive – and dependent – relationships with information technologies, it seems inevitable that leadership, too, should change.

It is perhaps too early to say to what extent this overlaps with Western's (2008) observations on the emergent eco-leadership discourse. Nevertheless, Western argues that 'Leadership becomes less about control and more about navigating through complex and diverse business eco-systems' (2008: 186).

Such navigation can be enabled through mental processes of free association, or triggered by experiences in nature, which serve to liberate the creativity and imagination and give rise to the 'unthought idea'. As Western says, 'For the highly rational management world, many of these ideas are challenging and truly create a new paradigm. How do you invest in a business whose leadership talks about not-knowing and emergence as strategy?' (2008: 196–197).

One of the frustrations sometimes voiced by participants who use scenario-planning processes is that they can leave participants with 'So what?' questions. Having mapped a set of potential futures, individual leaders can be left feeling powerless to act within worlds defined by external drivers over which they have little influence.

Senge et al. (2005) outline practical approaches that leaders can take to develop effectiveness in those seeking to work collaboratively to bring about change that starts with a process of sensing the future, then acting to create it together.

In attempting to identify new approaches to leading towards uncertain futures, Senge et al. stress the importance of suspending the 'Voice of Judgment' (2005: 30). They outline the three stages of what they call (because of its diagrammatic shape) the U Process: sensing, presencing, realizing – a deepening of prior understanding of learning processes (2005: 88). This involves intense observation until you become one with the world; retreat and reflection, allowing inner knowledge to emerge; 'act[ing] swiftly, with a natural flow'. Making this happen in organizational reality can result in 'everyone in the room . . . speaking from a deeper source' (2005: 95). It is also likely to lead to rapid prototyping of new ideas and services, thus working outside accepted norms of product cycles and lead times.

They cite an example of reflective, contemplative practices at staff meetings at high-technology company Intel, and how these led to a new plant going from start-up to full-volume production in a tiny proportion of the time expected or planned (2005: 142). These practices enabled slowing down and gaining an awareness of the environment in which staff found themselves, together with a sense of opening out to others. This resonates with a modern scientific worldview of the interconnectedness of everything – extending, of course, to the interconnectedness of people, and the accompanying responsibilities of leadership.

Temkin (2010) highlights the importance of purposeful leadership, with implications for universities of the importance of defining the institution's student experience and its 'touch points'. Such leadership can succeed, according to Temkin, only when leaders act consistently in pursuit of goals they espouse. If the touch points – every point of contact with the institution and its brand – are to make a high impact, they need to engage emotionally. The key measure of success in having achieved such engagement is in the extent to which students (and, of course, other clients such as businesses and social partners) are likely to recommend their experience to those close to them, defined by Reicheld (2003) in terms of the Net Promoter Score. Technology can be used to survey views of engagement at many points of contact, and an organization that is able to learn from and respond to such views places itself in a strong position of competitive advantage. Building relationships with detractors has been found (Gauntlett et al., 2012) to be influential in converting them to become promoters and advocates. Given that those with strong opinions are likely to share these using wide-ranging digital channels, investing effort in relationships is a key task of institutional leaders.

Given the scale and pace of change anticipated by Barber et al. (2013), the importance of those qualities of leadership that are defined by learning appears to be growing exponentially. Here is the challenge as set out in the IPPR's report *An Avalanche is Coming*:

> University leaders need to take control of their own destiny and seize the opportunities open to them through technology . . . to provide broader,

deeper and more exciting education. Leaders will need to have a keen eye toward creating value for their students.

(Barber et al., 2013: 5)

By 2020, the role of learning in leadership will have moved to centre stage. According to Fairhurst (2008: 32), the challenges of cultural inclusion, creative adaptation and customer integration will have increased substantially. The skills base will have shifted to place greater emphasis on managing virtual teams, while leaders may controversially find themselves drawing on pharmaceutical enhancers in order to boost their cognitive and emotional intelligences.

Leaders will need to have evolved a mature sense of their own leadership identities that goes considerably further than the notions of self-awareness that form the basis of many programmes of personal and professional development. They will have drawn on a broad canvas of learning opportunities (including stretch assignments, cultural challenge tasks, internships and secondments) that extend beyond the limits of formal instruction based in training rooms. As a result, there may be more abundant examples in the higher education sector of true learning organizations.

CASE STUDY 15: CURTIN UNIVERSITY
Leadership development

Background

A longstanding priority has been given to leadership and leadership development at Curtin University. This was articulated in a case study by Murray (2011) that outlines the 20-year history of Curtin's internationalization plans and the leadership development necessary to embed the internationalizing of the curriculum and research, staff exchange, student mobility and cultural variety and the establishment of offshore developments. This case study concludes with the statement:

> The success of Curtin Sarawak is a reflection of a wide range of factors that the Curtin leadership was able to comprehend and master at the critical first stage of development of the partnership. Hard and soft skills and capabilities of many individual leaders and managers in Australia and in Sarawak came into play to achieve the desired outcome. Without these capabilities the project would not have succeeded. It is a reflection of the strong and capable leadership in Curtin at the time that this was understood and successfully acted on, despite the pressures imposed by the timeframe for delivery.

As a complement to the internationalization developments and the existing leadership skills of the senior staff within the university, Curtin University

---

undertook research to identify the current capabilities and competencies of academic staff within the institution. The report by Scott et al. (2008) reviewed the leadership and management skills necessary for course leaders and derived not only a set of competencies but also capabilities that course (programme) leaders should possess (see Table 7.7). These leadership competencies and capabilities were used by Curtin University to initiate its own research, and an internal project was set up to design and implement a leadership development programme for all course (programme) leaders.

Table 7.7 Competencies and capabilities of programme leaders

Competence	Capability
Relevant skills and knowledge that are delivered to a set standard in a specific context	Ability to figure out when and when not to deploy these competencies, and a capacity to refine, update and develop them
Ability to deliver/perform	Ability to learn
Performance	Creativity
Ability to deliver set tasks in specific and relatively predictable situations	Ability to deliver new approaches in complex, uncertain situations
A focus on the present	A focus on the future
Working productively and efficiently in situations that are stable	Working productively with instability and change

The aim of the project was to develop and trial an experiential academic leadership programme designed to enhance the leadership skills of course coordinators to enable them ultimately to improve the student experience of learning. The project was to cover 55 academic staff in total, and included the development of several products including:

1 a project report
2 10 modules with capacity for adaptations suitable for different university environments, including face-to-face, fully online or blended delivery
3 a guide to the coordination and facilitation of programmes
4 an extensive package of programme resources including over 100 pre-programme, programme and post-programme items
5 a dissemination website.

The integrating, competing values framework

A framework (Vilkinas and Cartan, 2006) for reviewing each of the programme leaders in a 360-degree appraisal, and an assessment of how they preferred to work in a team, had been developed and researched nationally in Australia. This was used as a key mechanism within Curtin University for the course leaders so that they gained a perspective on how they were viewed by their line managers, peers, and the people with whom they worked on their programme.

Outcome

Curtin University has found it beneficial to develop leadership skills throughout the organization. The development of the leadership materials and the use of the Integrated Competing Values Framework tool facilitated the leadership development of this key group of staff within the institution, improved the quality of delivery and enhanced the student experience.

Questions

1   How does your university take forward leadership development and ensure it aligns with the strategy and overall priorities of the institution?
2   Are competencies and capabilities appropriate as a guide for this level of leader?
3   How does leadership development at this level occur within your institution?

Case study developed by Sue Jones, Curtin University, Perth, Australia and Professor Dawn Forman.

References

Agness, L. (2013) *Change your Life with NLP* (New York: Skyhorse Publishing).

Ainscow, M., Hopkins, D., Southworth, G. and M. West (1994) *Creating the Conditions for School Improvement* (London: David Fulton).

Anderson, L. (2003) 'A Leadership Approach to Managing People in Education' in L. Kydd, L. Anderson and W. Newton (eds) *Leading People and Teams in Education* (London: Sage).

Baddeley, S. and James, K. (1987) 'Owl, Fox, Donkey, Sheep: Political Skills for Managers', *Management Education and Development*, 18(1), 3–19.

Barber, M., Donnelly, K. and Rizvi, S. (2013) *An Avalanche is Coming* (London: Institute for Public Policy Research).

Behrendt, L. (1996) *Aboriginal Dispute Resolution: A Step towards Self Determination and Community Autonomy* (Annandale: Federation Press).

Belbin, R.M. (2010) *Team Roles at Work*, 2nd edn. (Oxford: Butterworth-Heinemann).

Bessant, W., Hughes, T. and Richards, S. (2010). *Beyond Light Bulbs and Pipelines: Leading and Nurturing Innovation in the Public Sector* (Ascot: Sunningdale Institute).

Bolden, R., Gosling, J., O'Brien, A., Peters, K. and Haslam, A. (2012) *Academic leadership: Changing Conceptions, Identities and Experiences in UK Higher Education* (London: Leadership Foundation for Higher Education).

Bolden, R., Petrov, G. and Gosling, J. (2008) *Developing Collective Leadership in Higher Education* (London: Leadership Foundation for Higher Education).

Botsman, R. and Rogers, R. (2011) *What's Mine is Yours: How Collaborative Consumption is Changing the Way We Live* (London: Collins).

Bourdieu, P. (2008) *Sketch for a Self-Analysis* (Chicago: Chicago University Press).

Bryman, A. (2007) *Effective Leadership in Higher Education: An Analysis of the Research Literature from Various Sectors* (London: Leadership Foundation for Higher Education).

Buckingham, M. (2007) *Go Put Your Strengths to Work: 6 Powerful Steps to Achieve Outstanding Performance* (London: Simon and Schuster).

Cabinet Office (2009, July) *Review of Public Service Leadership Development* (unpublished draft) (London: Cabinet Office).

Cabinet Office (2013) *The Coalition: Together in the National Interest* (London: HMSO).

Carbon Trust (2006) *Introducing Higher Education Carbon Management*. www.carbontrust.co.uk/Publications/pages/publicationdetail.aspx?id=PAC046

Chickering, A.W. and Gamson, Z.F. (1987) *Seven Principles for Good Practice in Undergraduate Education* (Racine, WI : The Johnson Foundation).

Clutterbuck, A. and Megginson, D. (2006) Making Coaching Work: Creating a Coaching Culture (London: Chartered Institute of Personnel and Development).

Coffin, J. M. (2007) 'Rising to the Challenge in Aboriginal Health by Creating Cultural Security', *Aboriginal & Islander Health Worker Journal*, 31(3), 22–24.

Collini, S. (2012) *What Are Universities for?* (Rickmansworth: Penguin).

Crisp, N. (2010) *Turning the World Upside Down: The Search for Global Health in the 21st Century* (London: The Royal Society of Medicine).

Critchley, B. (2010) 'Relational Coaching: Taking the Coaching High Road', *Journal of Management Development*, 29(10), 851–863.

DBIS (2010a) *Skills for Sustainable Growth* (London: Department for Business and Innovation).

DBIS (2010b) *Securing a Sustainable Future for Higher Education* (London: Department for Business and Innovation).

DBIS (2010c) *Higher Education Funding for 2011–12 and Beyond* (Letter to Higher Education Funding Council for England, 20 December).

DBIS (2011) *Students at the Heart of the System* (London: Department for Business, Innovation and Skills).

De Haan, E. and Blass, E. (2007) 'Using Critical Moments to Learn about Coaching', *Ashridge Training Journal*, April, 54–58.

Department for Education and Skills (2003) *The Future of Higher Education* (London: Department for Education and Skills).

Diamond, I. (2011) *Efficiency and Effectiveness in Higher Education: A Report by the Universities UK Efficiency and Modernisation Task Group* (London: Universities UK).

Doz, Y. and Kosonen, M. (2008) *Fast Strategy: How Strategic Agility Will Help You Stay Ahead of the Game* (Harlow: Pearson Education).

Ernst, C., Hannum, K.M. and Ruderman, M.N. (2010) 'Developing Intergroup Leadership' in E. Van Velsor, C.D. McCauley and M.N. Ruderman (eds) *A Handbook of Leadership Development* (San Francisco: Jossey-Bass).

Evans, K., Hodkinson, P., Rainbird, H. and Unwin, L. (2006) *Improving Workplace Learning* (London: Routledge).

Fairhurst, P. (2008) *Learning and Development 2020: Exploring the Future of Workplace Learning, Phase 1 Report* (Brighton: Institute for Employment Studies).

Fielding, M. and Bragg, S. (2003) *Students as Researchers: Making a Difference* (Harlow: Pearson Education).

Forman, D., Jones, M. and Thistlethwaite, J. (eds) (2014) *Leadership Development for Interprofessional Education and Collaborative Practice* (London: Palgrave Macmillan).

Forman, D., Joyce, M. and McMahon, G. (2013) *Creating a Coaching Culture for Managers in Your Organisation* (London: Routledge).

Fullan, M. (2001) *Leading in a Culture of Change* (San Francisco: Jossey-Bass).

Fullan, M. and Scott, M. (2009) *Turnaround Leadership for Higher Education* (San Francisco: Jossey-Bass).

Garrett, G. and Davies, G.D. (2010) *Herding Cats: Being Advice to Aspiring Academic and Research Leaders* (Axminster: Triarchy Press).

Gauntlett, D., Ackermann, E., Whitebread, D., Wolbers, T., Weckstrom, C. and Stjerne Thomsen, B. (2012) *The Future of Learning* (Billund: LEGO Learning Institute).

Gentle, P. (2010) 'The Influence of an Action Learning Set of Affective and Organizational Cultural Factors', *Action Learning Research and Practice*, 9(1), 17–28.

Gibbs, G. (2010) *Dimensions of Quality* (York: Higher Education Academy).

Gibbs, G., Knapper, C. and Piccinin, S. (2009) *Departmental Leadership of Teaching in Research-Intensive Environments* (London: Leadership Foundation for Higher Education).

Gitsham , M. (2012) *Developing Leaders Who Create Value Sustainability* (Ashridge: Ashridge Business School).

Goddard, J. (2009) *Re-inventing the Civic University* (London: NESTA).

Goleman, D. (1995) *Emotional Intelligence* (New York: Bantam).

Goleman, D., Boyatzis, R. and Mckee, A. (2002) *Primal Leadership: Learning to Lead with Emotional Intelligence* (Cambridge, MA: Harvard Business School Press).

Goold, S. (2006) 'Getting 'em 'n' Keepin' 'em: Indigenous Issues in Nursing Education', *Australian Aboriginal Studies*, 2, 57–61.

Graham, S., Lester, N. and Dickerson, C. (2012) 'Discover – Deepen – Do: A 3-D Pedagogical Approach for Developing Newly Qualified Teachers as Professional Learners', *Australian Journal of Teacher Education*, 37(9), 3.

Grint, K. (2005) *Leadership: Limits and Possibilities* (Basingstoke: Palgrave Macmillan).

Grint, K. (2010) *Leadership: A Very Short Introduction* (Oxford: Oxford University Press).

Hargreaves, A. and Harris, A. (2011) *Performance beyond Expectations* (Nottingham: NCSL).

Harvey, L. and Knight, P. (1996) *Transforming Higher Education* (Buckingham: Society for Research into Higher Education/Open University Press).

Hawkins, P. and Smith, N. (2011) *Coaching, Mentoring and Organisational Consultancy: Supervision and Development* (London: Routledge).

Hawkins, P. and Winter, J. (1997) *Mastering Change: Learning the Lessons of the Enterprise in Higher Education Initiative* (Sheffield: Department for Education and Employment).

HEFCE (2010a) *Evaluation of the Leadership Foundation for Higher Education* (Bristol: HEFCE).

HEFCE (2010b) *Taking the Pulse of an Institution: A HEFCE Leadership Governance and Management Fund Project* (Bristol: HEFCE).

Heifetz, R., Grashow, A. and Linsky, M. (2009). *The Practice of Adaptive Leadership: Tools and Tactics for Changing Your Organization and the World* (Cambridge, MA: Harvard Business School Publishing).

Helms, J.E. (1990) 'Toward a Model of White Racial Identity Development' in *Black and White Racial Identity: Theory, Research and Practice* (pp. 49–66) (New York: Greenwood Press).

Hockey, J. and Ley I. (2010) *Leading for Engagement: How Senior Leaders Engage Their People* (Sunningdale: National School of Government).

Hofstede, G. (1980) *Culture's Consequences* (Beverly Hills, CA: Sage).

ILERN (2007) *Positive Leadership: Thinking and Rethinking Leadership* (Nottingham: National College for School Leadership).

Johnson, G., Scholes, K. and Whittington, R. (2008) *Exploring Corporate Strategy* (Harlow: Pearson Education).

Kegan, R. and Lahey, L. (2009) *Immunity to Change* (Boston: Harvard Business School).

Kellerman, B. (2012) *The End of Leadership* (New York: Harper Collins).

Kennie, T. (2012) *Disruptive Innovation and the Higher Education Ecosystem Post-2012* (London: Leadership Foundation for Higher Education).

Kennie, T. and Woodfield, S. (2008) *The Composition, Challenges and Changes in the Top Team Structures of UK Higher Education Institutions* (London: Leadership Foundation for Higher Education).

King, S.N. and Santana, L.C. (2010) 'Feedback-Intensive Programs' in E. Van Velsor, C.D. McCauley and M.N. Ruderman (eds) *A Handbook of Leadership Development* (San Francisco: Jossey-Bass).

Kline, N. (1999) *Time to Think: Listening to Ignite the Human Mind* (London: Cassell).

Latin America Current Events and News (2011) *Colombia, 90% of Universidad de la Sabana Flooded*. http://latinamericacurrentevents.com/colombia-90-universidad-de-la-sabana-flooded

Leadbeater, C. and Mongon, D. (2008) *Leadership for Public Value: Achieving Valuable Outcomes for Children, Families and Communities* (Nottingham: NCSL).

Leadership Foundation for Higher Education/Cardiff University (2011) *Lean Management: Doing More with Less* (London: Leadership Foundation for Higher Education).

Leadership Foundation for Higher Education (2013) Unpublished survey of senior leaders engaging in the Changing the Learning Landscape programme.

Lipman-Blumen, J. (2005). *The Allure of Toxic Leaders: Why We Follow Destructive Bosses and Corrupt Politicians – And How We Can Survive Them* (New York: Oxford University Press).

Lofthouse, R., Leat, D. and Towler, C. (2010) *Coaching for Teaching and Learning: A Practical Guide for Schools* (Reading: CfBT Education Trust).

Lumby, J. (2012) *What Do We Know about Leadership?* (London: Leadership Foundation for Higher Education).

Maastricht University (2010) *Corporate Report: Leading in Learning: Where Research and Teaching are Complementary* (Maastricht: Maastricht University).

Macleod, D. and Clarke, N. (2009) *Engaging for Success* (London: Office of Public Sector Information).

Mabey, C. and Iles, P. (1989) *Managing Learning* (Milton Keynes: Open University Press).

Maddock, S. (2009) *Change You Can Believe In* (Ascot: Whitehall Innovation Hub).

McBeath, J., Oduro, G.K.T. and Waterhouse, J. (2004) *Distributed Leadership in Action: A Study of Current Practice in Schools* (Nottingham: National College for School Leadership).

McCaffery, P. (2010) *The Higher Education Manager's Handbook* , 2nd ed. (London: RoutledgeFalmer).

McNay, I. (1995) 'From the Collegial Academy to Corporate Enterprise: The Changing Cultures of Universities', in T. Schuller (ed.) *The Changing University?* Buckingham: Open University Press, pp. 105–115.

Middlehurst, R. (1993) *Leading Academics* (Buckingham: Society for Research into Higher Education/Open University Press).

Mowles, C., van der Gaag, A. and Fox, J. (2010) 'The Practice of Complexity: Review, Change and Service Improvement in an NHS Department', *Journal of Health Organization and Management*, 24(2), 127–144.

Mulgan, G. (2010) *The Birth of the Relational State* (London: The Young Foundation).

Murray, D. (2011) 'Curtin University, Australia and the State Government of Sarawak, Malaysia Case Study' in J. Fielden (ed.) *Research and Development Series: Leadership and Management of International Partnerships* (London: Leadership Foundation for Higher Education).

Nayar, V. (2010) *Employees First, Customers Second* (Boston: Harvard Business School Publishing).

NCSL (2005a) *Success and Sustainability – Developing the Strategically-Focused School* (Nottingham: NCSL).

NCSL (2005b) *70,000 Heads Are Better than One – Lessons from the World's Largest Online Learning Community for School Leaders* (Nottingham: NCSL).

NCSL (2006) *Professional Learning Communities* (Nottingham: NCSL).

Passfield, R. (2002) 'Creating Innovation and Synergy through a Parallel Action Learning Structure', *The Learning Organization*, 9(4), 150–158.

Pearl, D. (2012) *Will There Be Doughnuts?* (London: HarperCollins).

Pedler, M., Burgoyne, J. and Boydell, T. (1991). *The Learning Company: A Strategy for Sustainable Development.* (New York: McGraw-Hill).

Raelin, J. (2003) *The Leaderful Fieldbook: Strategies and Activities for Developing Leadership in Everyone* (New York: Davies-Black Publishing).

Raelin, J. (2010) *Creating Leaderful Organisations – How to Bring Out Leadership in Everyone* (San Francisco: Berret-Koehler).

Ramsden, P. (1998) *Learning to Lead in Higher Education* (London: Routledge).

Ranking Web of World Universities (2011) http://www.webometrics.info/premierleague.html

Reicheld, F. (2003) 'The One Number You Need to Grow', *Harvard Business Review*, 81, December, 46–54.

Revans, R. (1983) *ABC of Action Learning.* Bromley: Chartwell-Bratt.

Robinson, D. (2008, 2nd edition) *Unconditional Leadership* (London: Community Links).

Rooke, D. and Torbert, W.R. (2005) 'Seven Transformations of Leadership', *Harvard Business Review*, April, 1–11.

Rubin, B.D. (2007) *Excellence in Higher Education* (Washington, DC: NACUBO). http://oirap.rutgers.edu/msa/documents/eheguide5-29.pdf

Rudd, K. (2008) *Apology to Australia's Indigenous Peoples* (speech delivered at the House of Representatives, Parliament of Australia, 13 February.

Ryde, R. (2007) *Thought Leadership* (Basingstoke: Palgrave Macmillan).

Ryde, R. (2013) *Never Mind the Bosses – Hastening the Death of Deference for Business Success* (San Francisco: Jossey-Bass).

Savin-Baden, M. (2000) *Problem-Based Learning in Higher Education: Untold Stories* (Buckingham: SRHE/Open University Press).

Scott, G., Coates H. and Anderson, M. (2008) *Learning Leaders in Times of Change: Academic Leadership Capabilities for Australian Higher Education* (Chippendale: Australian Learning and Teaching Council).

Senge, P. (1990) *The Fifth Discipline: The Art and Practice of the Learning Organization* (London: Doubleday).

Senge, P., Scharmer, C.O., Jaworkski, J. and Flowers, B.S. (2005) *Presence: Exploring Profound Change in People, Organisations and Society* (London: Nicholas Brealey Publishing).

Shaw, C. (2007) *The DNA of Customer Experience: How Emotions Drive Value* (Basingstoke: Palgrave Macmillan).

Stacey, R. (2013) Talk given to participants on Strategic Change Programme run by the Leadership Foundation for Higher Education, 10 April.

Stein, S.J. and Book, H. (2006) *The EQ Edge: Emotional Intelligence and Your Success* (San Francisco: Jossey-Bass).

TDA (2007) *School Improvement Planning Toolkit* (London: Teacher Development Agency).

Temkin, B. (2010) *Mapping the Customer Journey* (Cambridge, MA: Forrester Research).

Thomas, K.W. and Kilmann, R.H. (1974). *Thomas-Kilmann Conflict Mode Instrument* (Mountain View, CA: Xicom).

Tourish, D. (2012) *Leadership Development within the UK Higher Education System: Its Impact on Organisational Performance, and the Role of Evaluation* (London: Leadership Foundation for Higher Education).

Tuckman, B.W. (1965) 'Developmental Sequence in Small Groups', *Psychological Bulletin*, 63, 384–399 (Bethesda, MD: Naval Medical Research Institute).

Tysome, T. (2013) *Higher Education Talking Heads: Leading Academic Talent to a Successful Future* (unpublished paper commissioned by the Leadership Foundation for Higher Education).

United Nations (2007) *Population Prospects, 2006 Revision*, ESA/P/WP.202, p. 19 (New York: UN).

Universities UK (2011) *Efficiency Exchange*. www.universitiesuk.ac.uk/aboutus/AssociatedOrganisations/Pages/EfficiencyExchange.aspx

University of Birmingham/Homes & Communities Agency (2011) *Leadership of Place – Transforming Communities by Changing the Way We Lead* (Birmingham: Birmingham Business School).

Vaillancourt, A.M. (2012) Creating a Community of Leaders. *Higher Education Workplace*, Winter 2012/13, 31, 34–6.

Vilkinas, T. and Cartan, G. (2006) The Integrated Competing Values Framework: Its Special Configuration. *Journal of Management Development*, 25(6), 505–521.

Wagstaff, D. (2013) *Collaborations and Partnerships in Higher Education* (London: Leadership Foundation for Higher Education).

Wang, C.L. and Ahmed, P.K. (2002) *A Review of the Concept of Organisational Learning* (Telford: Wolverhampton Business School Management Research Centre).

Ward, H. (2013) 'Magnify Students' Research Skills', *tespro*, 2(30), 4–7 (London: TSL Education).

Watson, D. (2009) *The Question of Morale: Managing Happiness and Unhappiness in University Life* (Maidenhead: McGraw-Hill).

Wenger, E. (1998) *Communities of Practice: Learning, Meaning and Identity* (Cambridge: Cambridge University Press).

West-Burnham, J. and Ireson, J. (2005) *Leadership Development & Personal Effectiveness* (Nottingham: NCSL).

Western, S. (2008) *Leadership: A Critical Text* (London: Sage).

Whitmore, J. (1992) *Coaching for Performance* (London: Nicholas Brealy).

Wikipedia (2013a) http://en.wikipedia.org/wiki/Colombia

Wikipedia (2013b) http://en.wikipedia.org/wiki/University_of_La_Sabana

Woods, P.A. (2003) Democratic Leadership: Drawing Distinctions with Distributed Leadership. *International Journal of Leadership in Education*, 6(1), 3–26.

Zepke, N. (2007) Leadership, Power and Activity Systems in a Higher Education Context: Will Distributive Leadership Serve in an Accountability-Driven World? *International Journal of Leadership in Education*, 10(3), 301–314.

Index